T0342606

Psychomanagement:

AN AUSTRALIAN AFFAIR

Robert Spillane

GOKO PUBLISHING

GOKO Management and Publishing
PO Box 7109
McMahons Point 2060
Sydney, Australia

Library of Congress Cataloging-in-Publication Data

Spillane, Robert
    Psychomanagement: An Australian Affair
    p. cm.
    ISBN: 978-1-61339-903-3 (pbk.)

CONTENTS

ACKNOWLEDGEMENTS

This book is a revised edition of *The Rise of Psychomanagement in Australia* (Melbourne: Michelle Anderson Publishing, 2011).

The quotations at the beginning of each chapter are from *The Management Contradictionary* by Benjamin Marks, Rodney Marks and Robert Spillane (Michelle Anderson Publishing, 2006). I thank my co-authors for permission to reproduce our work.

Several chapters contain material from published articles and book chapters. I am grateful for the editors and publishers of the journals and books in which these pieces appeared for granting permission for selective reproduction.

Chapter 3: 'Definitely Drucker,' AFR Boss, March, 2008.

Chapter 7: 'Medicalising Work Behaviour: The Case of Repetition Strain Injury,' *Asia Pacific Journal of Human Resources*, 2008, 46, 1, pp. 85-99.

I am grateful to Lenore Grunsell for allowing me to work from the unpublished manuscripts of her late husband and my friend and co-author, John Martin.

Finally, I thank Katherine at GOKO Publishing for agreeing to publish new and old material on a controversial subject. This book is dedicated to her.

PROLOGUE

Mythology: The foundation of the management profession, undermined by comparison with real professions, such as banking, gambling and witchcraft.

Twenty managers spend five days at a management training centre. They are there, at great expense, to acquire spiritual intelligence from their executive coach. The first two days are devoted to 'energy transference': the coach transfers her spiritual intelligence to the managers who spend the next two days transferring it to each other. The litmus test of their success in sharing this new-age intelligence with each other is fire-walking. At the end of an excruciating week of psychobabble, each manager is invited to defy the laws of physics by walking across hot coals. All managers meekly obey and suffer serious burns. Most are removed to the local hospital and one is found sitting in a toilet with his feet in a bucket of water.

At a management school, managers have 'lunatic' written on their foreheads. They are at the mercy of a 'facilitator' who lives in a new age world of natural energy and believes that managers should get in touch with nature. They are taken to a lake and told to bow and thank nature (and the lake) for its largesse. Later that night, amazed witnesses try to make sense of adult human beings howling at the moon. They conclude that the managers are seriously overpaid and possibly mad. They wonder why they are paid at all.

Another training centre specialises in assessing managers' personalities. One brave manager resists and is immediately labelled a 'difficult personality'. A colleague submits to the personality test and is ordered to wear his 'personality' on his shirt for five days. He objects but complies. One week later he initiates legal action against those who subjected him to psychological indignities.

What do these cases have to do with management or the training of managers? They are, I suggest, distractions from the traditional practice of management because the ultimate test of management is performance: the achievement of actual results.

Managers get their authority from their technical expertise and their rhetorical skills. When managers and colleagues interact, they attempt to influence each other to see or do things. The persuasive element in the relationship is what qualifies the actions of one or both parties as fundamentally rhetorical.

Today, rhetoric has a negative connotation, identified with the vacuous jargon of politicians and corporate executives. Yet it was not always so. The ancient Greeks valued noble over base rhetoric, a distinction which depends on whether rhetoricians are judged to influence others toward what is good or what is bad: a judgement that will differ according to the values of those who render it.

Managerial authority is grounded, in large part, on noble rhetoric: communications requesting obedience, which are supported by *reasons* why the action is the desirable one. As reasoning means the ability to argue effectively about relevant matters, authoritative managers are those who offer valid reasons for a proposed course of action. Consequently, competent employees earn the right to argue with their managers. This consequence is neither obvious nor acceptable to many managers who view argument and debate as a challenge to their authority. Authoritative managers embrace and authoritarians reject argument and debate.

In Australia it is dangerous to appear to be authoritarian: the bitter pill of power needs to be sugar-coated. This is where soft-skill management enters the picture in a suitably disguised, if not Machiavellian, form.

In the postmodern world of management, arguing is a career-limiting activity. Individuals who argue with their managers are likely to be accused of lacking the 'soft-skills' of management. In some cases, they are judged to have a low level of 'emotional intelligence'. In more extreme cases, they are considered to be suffering from a personality disorder.

The popularity of soft-skill management in Australia has redefined management and created *psychomanagers*: managers who manage by personality. I use the term 'personality' broadly to include personality traits, psychological motives, and various forms of 'intelligence': cognitive; emotional; moral; and spiritual. Influenced by new age lunacy, postmodern preciousness, political correctness and feminism, management training has become a standing joke among those who want to be judged on actual results and not on their often difficult personalities.

The rise of psychomanagement has spawned a cult of personality that subjects individuals to psychometric tests in the mistaken belief that certain personalities make bad managers and others make good managers, and even leaders. But managers and leaders occupy mutually antagonistic roles and the shift from one to the other is fraught with danger. The manager's authority is based on role and the leader's is based on personal attraction. Given the behaviour of leaders in the twentieth century, many people have concluded that it is dangerous to follow individuals because of personality, 'vision' or 'mission'. History tells us, or most of us, that if we follow leaders we are likely to end up in chains behind them.

Using psychology to manage others has great attraction because it offers managers the means by which they can control their colleagues. The problem is that psychomanagement requires knowledge and skills that managers don't have. When managers become psychomanagers they have to gain insight into the inner lives of their colleagues, understand various personality theories, tests and therapies. Failing this, they yield their authority to counsellors, coaches or consultants who cannot agree on the basic assumptions about human behaviour. And when they try to apply psychomanagement, they undermine their authority because the relationships of psychologist and client and of manager and subordinate colleague are mutually exclusive.

Psychomanagement combines attention to performance and an obsession with personality and an assumption that the two are linked. They are not. Nevertheless, psychomanagers continue to promote the view, discredited by sixty years of research, that personality predicts managerial performance. Furthermore, psychologists cannot agree on even the most fundamental principles of personality. Behaviourists and existentialists argue against the existence of personality traits, and psychoanalysts claim they cannot be assessed by psychometric tests.

Managers who find the task of making employees' strengths productive too onerous emphasise employees' weaknesses. Their attempt to eliminate employees' personal deficiencies encourages them to practice counselling in which they are not trained – and neglect skills in which they are. Once they embrace therapeutic counselling, the roles of manager and counsellor collide. Their point of intersection represents one of the major challenges for Australian managers who are required by occupational health and safety legislation to provide an occupational environment adapted for the physiological and *psychological* needs of employees. Clearly, those who want to manage by performance have had their waters muddied.

The popularity in Australian management of personality, motivation, bonding, emotional and moral intelligence raises interesting questions about the changing face of management. How did it come to pass that managers today are expected to 'bond' by howling at the moon, or walking on fire to demonstrate their 'spiritual' ability to defy the laws of physics? How did new age spiritualism, folk psychology and soft-skill management become part of the practice of management? Or, as the ancient Romans asked, *Cui bono*?

Traditionally, the role of psychology was to provide the opportunity for individuals to master themselves, not to manipulate others. Originally known as moral philosophy, psychology defended the maxim 'know and master yourself'. As we shall see, psychologists have been welcomed into Australian management: some work *with* managers to encourage them to master themselves; others work *for* managers to encourage them to master others.

Australian managers are told that they should be managers and leaders, managers and mates, managers and mentors. They are told that they need coaches, consultants and counsellors. When they were confronted with 'epidemics' of Repetition Strain Injury, occupational stress, personality disorders and mental illnesses, many concluded that managing in Australia is a challenging business.

This book, then, is about Australian managers, their long-standing affair with psychologists, and the rise of the psychomanager. It is written by an Australian academic who for half a century has studied, taught and consulted with managers and participated in several of the social movements in which they have been embroiled. It is therefore a personal, selective, account of a professional life spent studying the problematic relationship between managers and psychologists.

1

A WEIRD COUNTRY

Egalitarianism: The belief that all subordinates should submit equally.

One of Australia's glorious sisters, Miles Franklin, noted that one of its brilliant sons, Henry Lawson, called Australia the paradise of mediocrity and the grave of genius. She advised visitors who become perplexed by its contradictions and inverted emphases to soak themselves in its atmosphere before arriving at dogmatic conclusions.[1]

English novelist D.H. Lawrence did not live long enough to benefit from Franklin's advice. He visited Sydney in 1922, stayed for three months, and wrote one of his worst novels – *Kangaroo* – which included wonderful descriptions of the Australian landscape and hilarious descriptions of Australian manners. Lawrence described Australia as 'a weird, big country. It feels so empty and untrodden...This is the most democratic place I have *ever* been in. And the more I see of democracy the more I dislike it...You *never* knew anything so *nothing*...They are always vaguely and meaninglessly on the go. And it all seems so empty, so nothing, it almost makes you sick. They are healthy, and to my thinking almost imbecilic. That's what life in a new country does to you: it makes you so material, so *outward*, that your real inner life and your inner self dies out, and you clatter round like so many mechanical animals...I feel if I lived in Australia for ever I should never open my mouth once to say one word that meant anything. Yet they are very trustful and kind and quite competent in their jobs. There's no need to lock your doors, nobody will come and steal. All the outside life is so *easy*. But there it ends. There's nothing else...Nobody is any better than anybody else, and it really is democratic. But it all feels so slovenly, slip-shod, rootless and empty, it is like a dream...There is this for it, that here one doesn't feel the depression and the tension of Europe. Everything is happy-go-lucky, and one couldn't *fret* about anything if one tried. One just doesn't care. And they are all like that. Au *fond* they don't care a straw about anything: except just their little egos. Nothing *really* matters... [2]

Australia is a land of paradoxes, inversions and sardonic humour. Its paradoxes are exasperating, its inversions frustrating and its humour invalidating: such is life for a people who value liberty and equality; egalitarianism and bureaucracy; achievement and failure; heroes and underdogs. Australians aggressively insist on the dignity and importance of the individual but do their utmost to eliminate 'tall poppies'. Males are said to stick by their mates but will criticise them the moment their backs are turned. Females are said to be tough-minded but immerse themselves in the sentimental banality of women's magazines. Friendly and tolerant, Australians are laconic. Or are they merely apathetic? After all, they repeatedly tell each other: 'No worries'.

These paradoxes are combined with a notable inversion: historically Australians adopted a cynical attitude to so-called leaders – especially politicians, government bureaucrats and business managers – and made them the object of sardonic humour. The Australian way is that of the quiet achiever supported by a gospel of relaxation which emphasises getting on with, rather than dominating others; it is far more subtle than most observers and commentators care to discover, let alone acknowledge. Valuing their quality of life, Australians work quietly to secure it by defending a status quo that has given them advantages which are, they insist, second to none. Since they see their work as relatively unrelated to local luxuries – the weather, beaches and the vast open spaces – they are not obsessively concerned about economic performance. As for long-term planning, well, in the long-term we're all dead. In Australia the quo truly has status.

The Australian character of the nineteenth century was a mixture of Protestant, Catholic and Enlightenment values. But coursing through the veins of white Australians was European Romanticism. The most popular books in the early days of the colony were romantic: the novels of Sir Walter Scott for instance. As the decades passed romanticism developed an Australian flavour. The bush and bushrangers, the people of the outback, and common soldiers at Gallipoli were romanticised and passed into folklore. No doubt this romanticism had strong links to Irish mythology, but it also had important connections with English and German Romanticism. And while Australians would seem unlikely candidates for the label 'romantic,' this influence, although overlaid with laconic self-mockery, runs deep in the Australian character.

Nowadays it is considered politically incorrect to search for or talk about an Australian character since this merely reveals a portrait of dead, white, Anglo-Celtic males. And now that Australia is a multicultural society, it is considered mischievous and morally repugnant to emphasise the virtues (if any) of such a privileged, once-powerful group which dominated the virtuous citizenry. The fact remains, however, that Australian management in the twenty-first century shows the powerful influence of men and women from Anglo-Celtic backgrounds.

The early rulers of this country had to deal with Anglo/Celtic men and women who held sceptical, if not cynical, views about power, authority and political leadership (if such it can be called). This scepticism developed, in part, because Australians understood the negative consequences of allowing one's freedom to be surrendered to leaders, governors, politicians or policemen. Australians appreciate the reply of the army officer who was asked to rate a junior officer's 'leadership potential': 'I believe this officer has leadership potential,' the officer wrote, 'I believe his men would follow him anywhere, but it would be out of a sense of curiosity'.

Australians will follow pompous fools to watch them fall into error and then, with a wry smile, allow them to mend their ways. This is the local sport known as puncturing pomposity and pretentiousness, or 'cutting through the crap', and explains Australians' dislike of role-playing. They like to cut through the surface layer of role performance to get to the natural person. And natural men and women are, or should be, 'good blokes'. This approach to social relationships has earned them the vulgar tribute: they don't bullshit. Good blokes combine a down-to-earth, unpretentious, self-effacing demeanour with an unapologetic self-confidence. Australian poet Les Murray calls this character 'sprawl': loose-limbed in its mind, it leans on things. Its roots are Irish and it is the image of the Australian character: laconic, democratic and ironic. However, this emphasis on under-stated achievement is often misunderstood or denied, especially if Australians are judged by the sporting people who have adopted American manners.

The stereotypical Anglo-Celtic Australian appears to the outsider as relaxed to the point of apathy. Yet it is a watchful apathy since Australians live according to the 'silence of the law'. That beautiful phrase, coined by English philosopher Thomas Hobbes, describes the strength of liberal democracies: the respect for and internalisation of the law and its universal application. If the law is neither respected nor applied universally the result is tyranny. When the law is noisy the result is totalitarianism, or the sort of communitarianism that is inimical to most Australians. So when Australians are referred to as 'wallies' – lazy, self-interested hedonists – one learns to recognise the sound of competing values. It has to be said that in many countries the law is decidedly noisy.

In Australia the silence of the law is accompanied by the noise of celebrities. To be a celebrity, even if only for a day, is an American dream. It can be an Australian nightmare. To survive celebrity status in Australia one must appear to be unaffected by one's success. This means eschewing party politics, any form of formal authority, or support for any paranoid minority. In fact, it is wise to say very little and even wiser to control the temptation to put on a show for an audience, unless one is engaged in the activity (usually sport) for which one was originally recognised. Australians respect people who are artless, unsophisticated and unwilling to modify their behaviour for the social occasions that demand it. Their quiet confidence is supported by an almost wicked sense of humour, ironic, self-mocking, sentimental about family and close friends, and tough-mindedly realistic about the external world. And the external world in Australia is tough: the geography presents individuals with unbelievable challenges that usually end in heartbreak.

When free migrants arrived in the 1840s, many expected to work and master the land. It defeated them as it defeats everyone. But this defeat is the inspiration for much local poetry. Australians are not so callow as to be optimists about life in the bush. Not for them the view that life is, or ought to be, wonderful.

Beyond the cities and the coastal fringe, life is indescribably hard and gives rise to pessimism and even nihilism. But pessimism can be lamented and the lamentations are the very stuff of romantic poetry. And if nihilism is a dominant theme in the works of Henry Lawson and Joseph Furphy, it can be inspirational for those individuals confronted with the abyss who are determined to survive and overcome the tragedies of life.

If this sounds like the eccentric German philosopher Friedrich Nietzsche that is because Australia has had its Nietzscheans and some of them have said so: Norman Lindsay for example. Australians have developed their own brand of Nietzscheism, a tragic vitalism that, unlike Crocodile Dundee, does not win out in the end. The optimistic ending to modern travails points to the commercial motives of Hollywood. Life for battling Australians was tragic, thus the last Shakespearean words of Joseph Furphy (writing as Tom Collins, a government official of the ninth class) in his masterpiece, *Such is Life*:

> Now I had to enact the Cynic philosopher to Moriarty and Butler, and the aristocratic man with a 'past' to Mrs Beaudesart; with the satisfaction of knowing that each of these was acting a part to me. Such is life, my fellow mummers – just like a poor player, that bluffs and feints his hour upon the stage, and then cheapens down to mere nonentity. But let me not hear any small witticism to the further effect that its story is a tale told by a vulgarian, full of slang and blankly, signifying – nothing.[3]

According to Harry Heseltine, 'nothing' is a word which echoes throughout Australian literature. Presided over by Nietzsche, rather than Henry Lawson, Australian literature is based on a unique combination of glances into the pit and the erection of safety fences to prevent any falling in. If mateship dominates Lawson's and Furphy's writing, it is because behind it was an even more acute awareness of horror and emptiness. Mateship, egalitarian democracy, nationalism and realistic toughness can be seen as defences against the possibility of falling into the abyss. The main concern of early Australians was 'to acknowledge the terror at the basis of being, to explore its uses, and to build defences against its dangers'.[4]

Joseph Furphy described his brilliant novel about mateship, the bush and local characters as: temper, democratic; bias, offensively Australian. And so it is. *Such is Life* (and much Australian literature) is a study of role-playing and the absurdity of human endeavour. All the novel's characters are playing roles for other role-players. Society is a confidence trick which makes bearable the loneliness of the authentic life. The choice is between the best confidence trick and a confrontation with the abyss. Society is mostly bluff and bullying and those who succeed compromise themselves. Insincere role-players become sick at heart: many of the characters of Australian fiction and poetry are nauseated because their tough-minded realism is unable to contain the nihilism of Australian life.

Norman Lindsay countered the appalling emptiness of Australian life with a philosophy of 'creative effort' which combined the philosophies of Plato and Nietzsche (who do not mix easily). Nietzsche sought to transcend the Christian ethic of humility and compassion by affirming life itself which, in its natural form, is red in tooth and claw. The challenge for human beings is to sublimate their barbaric impulses, and create themselves as works of art.

In *Creative Effort*, written in 1920 after the senseless slaughter of the world war, Lindsay despaired of mankind. He believed that the only way some control might be exercised over man's destructive impulses was by restoring the great classical-romantic values in life and art that had been jettisoned in the early years of the twentieth century. Diagnosing modernist art as a symptom of a disease which was infecting Western civilisation, Lindsay refused to praise and admitted no merit in any modernist. They were 'mere savages' who, through their brutal representations, revealed their personal despair. Modernists are products of Europe's moral exhaustion and the neuroses engendered by the slaughter of the war: they have debased every classical value in art. He refused to believe that these 'fooleries' would last: people might be gullible but once the novelty wears off they will see through this monumental confidence trick. He was right about the gullibility but wrong about the demise of modernist art and literature. The rise of jazz infuriated him and he threatened to drive gramophone needles into the fingernails of every jazz producer in the land. He firmly believed that the nihilistic nature of modernism would ensure its early demise. But modernism triumphed and gave way to postmodernism and the decline of all aesthetic standards. Junk became art and the few remaining standards by which excellence was judged collapsed.

Lindsay's solution to the sickness of modernism rested with the artists who delved into unconscious life-forces to gain creative inspiration. Creative vision is the ability to discover one's own universality. But those who attempt this are doomed to failure. All we can do is engage in 'creative effort' and hope that there will be moments of aesthetic consciousness. Agreeing with the Romantics that although we can reject society we cannot ignore nature, Lindsay followed them in the belief that it is up to us to make nature sublime.

After acknowledging his profound debt to Nietzsche, Lindsay criticised him for attempting to create an earthly paradise built on the will of conquerors. Lindsay had no time for Nietzsche's idea that if the resentful mob cannot find a direction they must be given one. True, Nietzsche cleared away the rubbish that man had accumulated in building Western society. But having destroyed conventional Western values, Nietzsche fell into the trap of allowing himself to offer yet another version of the great Human State, lorded over by men of indomitable will who, believing that might is right, assume the right to impose themselves upon others in the name of creative leadership. Lindsay wanted nothing to do with that dangerous form of utopianism because it presupposed that power over others is given to those worthy of power. It never was, for those truly worthy of power disdained to use it.

In 1932 *Fortune* magazine in New York published Lindsay's opinions of Australians:

> The pose of the average Australian is that of a sardonic cocksureness. He is foolproof: aware of the rottenness of human motives and not to be taken in by them. He derides everything – except himself. His weekly papers reflect this uneasy vacillation of national self-esteem by their incessant jokes at the expense of Englishmen, who are exhibited as semi-imbeciles...In return, the Englishman dislikes the Australian as a colonial and a convict-bred upstart without any social status...
>
> Nevertheless, this annoying cocksureness of the Australian springs from two of his best virtues: his physical courage and his ability to think for himself in action. For a century he has been forcing a place for himself in a crude and difficult land

afflicted by drought and an uncertain rainfall, and the War of 1914 demonstrated his tradition of toughness and endurance. His sporting impulse is one outcome of his passion for taking a risk, whether on a bad horse or by dying of thirst, or casually swimming in the company of sharks...

Australian churches are almost empty; the Australian spends his Sunday rationally in the open air, and the Australian parsons have the hunted and harassed air of the uncertain wage-earner...

States of mind do not alter; they merely change their habitat. What *was* the parson and the convict official is now the bureaucrat. For its size, Australia has the largest bureaucracy with the lowest mentality in the world. The cost of maintaining the public service in Australia is such a joke that one can't laugh at it . . .

No one outside of Australia can have any notion of the degradation Australian intelligence has been subjected to by the antics of its official morons...[5]

Lindsay's philosophy is a form of cynical romanticism: it is libertarian, pessimistic, elitist, anti-authoritarian and it emphasises the individual's detachment from society and politics. His considerable influence on poets, novelists and playwrights, too many to list here, cannot be doubted. In our postmodern artistic world of junk, Lindsay is an anachronism and thus unjustly ignored.

By way of contrast, the Melbourne intellectual scene has been one of social, or even utopian, romanticism based on the view that art is central to society and a force for progressive social change. This view is anti-individualistic, egalitarian and socially democratic. In *Australian Cultural Elites*, John Docker argues that Melbourne intellectuals characteristically think that an Australian, nationalist-derived, social democratic ethos is compatible with what are viewed as the central values of European civilisation. Melbourne intellectuals feel at the centre of their society because they are modest social activists who strive to introduce Australia to European standards of sophistication.

Sydney intellectuals look to Europe as defining that which is important in life. But, Docker argues, they do not live in Europe, and if they did, would not feel part of Europe's social texture. Rejecting Australia and rejected by Europe, they are threatened by a personal nihilism. They opt for a third realm where universal romantic European ideals prevail. Since they reject society they cling to the romantic idea of the natural as real in life and the social as contingent. Melbourne romanticism embraces society; Sydney romanticism rejects it.

Lindsay's cynical romanticism was an aesthetic way of wrestling with existential dilemmas. Henry Lawson's was quite different. He recognised the need of man for man in a rough and brutalising country which produces profound feelings of emptiness. Faced with such absurd challenges to personal existence, it is tempting to withdraw into comfortable conformity. One can understand the need to invent the idea of mateship to counteract the consequences of widespread nihilism associated with life in the outback. Lawson obliged and so provided nineteenth-century frontier society with a survival technique and twentieth-century urban dwellers with one of their most cherished myths: mateship.

The loyalty of man to man is interwoven with an obsessive assertion of rights. But the passion for equal justice can easily sour into a grudge against gifted people and the desire for mateship can easily express itself by pulling down those who do not mix with the crowd. The ideal of mateship which appeals to ordinary Australians springs, not only from their eagerness to embrace fraternity, but from their determination to pull down high achievers.

In Lawson's life and work, however, mateship is fragile and conditional. It didn't (and still doesn't) apply to women, children, Aborigines and recent immigrants, although it did apply to dogs and horses. More importantly, Lawson realised that mateship was a protection against living with oneself. Those who deviate from the path of sociability and choose the lonely road of the reclusive individual invariably go mad. Did they need society? But it was the need to escape from the hypocrisy of society that made the journey to individuality necessary. And the result was, in Lawson's words, nothing.

Confronted by the terminal claustrophobia of hypocritical social relationships the inhabitants of this wide brown land had a unique opportunity to 'go bush'. Most didn't. And those who did – explorers, farmers, bushrangers – were generally broken by the bush. Their belief that coming to terms with the bush was an index of one's character reminds one again of Nietzsche: what doesn't kill one makes one stronger. To this day there is a silent and deep respect for those who battled with the bush and failed. Compassion for the underdog was not solely a reflection of identification with convicts and hostility towards their rulers. It had as much to do with the compassion and respect felt for those who struggled bravely but pointlessly with the harsh conditions of the Australian outback. Compassion for the underdog was combined with a romantic view of the people in the bush, even if our romantic writers were mostly disaffected urban intellectuals for whom the outback represented, as it does today, vicarious thrills and a relief from the claustrophobia and conformity of city and suburbs.

The vast open spaces of Australia influence people in different ways: they can be intoxicating for some, frightening for others. While 'Banjo' Paterson glorified life in the outback and wrote heroically optimistic tales, the poetry that plumbed the depths of the Australian character was cynically romantic. For many people the Australian landscape produces profound disquiet in which the individual is truly at one with a harsh, raw environment which so reduces him to insignificance that he feels swallowed up by nature. It is easy to understand why this experience was often portrayed by local writers as a form of madness and why Australians share a deep ambivalence towards the bush. Australians who know the bush acknowledge an intimate connection with each other: their empathy is based on a profound understanding of the precariousness of existence and the need of forbearance in the face of absurdity.

Australians, at least those in the outback, have faced a fundamental choice. One can act as if nothing matters or, while accepting the ultimate futility of life, one can act as if it is not futile. The Australian character has been moulded by this choice. And the result is a curious mixture of the two where today the most common expressions are 'no worries', 'she'll be right': cryptic and easy-going versions of Lawson's 'it doesn't matter much, nothing does'.

A darkly heroic realism developed among pioneers because of the harshness of the bush, which broke nearly all of the hard men and women who tried to master it. Thus there developed among the early Australians a creed of integrity – of being true to life – which reminds one of the cynical romanticism of Nietzsche and Albert Camus. Australian history is filled with tragic stories of lost children, drought, bushfire, floods, loneliness and tragic death in the outback. Australia boasts eleven of the fifteen most poisonous snakes in the world (including the top three); the most poisonous spider (and in Sydney too); the deadly box jelly-fish and blue-ringed octopus; scorpions; sting-rays, sharks; and crocodiles that have developed a taste for American tourists. And how does the man in the bush react to these nuisances?

> The first march of the young pioneers was over; the sixteen miles of rough uptrack had been traversed in a day; the average load had been over a hundred pounds per man . . . Between the wall of timber and the cliff rim ran an open strip a few yards wide, a breathing space which was chosen for a camp site. Before blankets were rolled out, six tiger snakes had to be killed and two bull-dog ants' nests burned out. Herb had been sitting on the brink of a cliff watching the opalescent spray of the falls leaping out into the twilight. On getting up to go back to the camp site, he found two hissing flattened reptiles blocking his path; there was no stick handy and no retreat. "Bring a stick!" he yelled to the others, "Two snakes here!" "You can have

my stick," Norb called out, a bit out of breath, "as soon as I've finished killing these beggars over here." Two carpet snakes and a twelve foot rock python were spared – they proved useful about the camp later by eradicating bush rats. It would have been a bad camp for a sleep-walker; three yards from the foot of their leafy beds was certain death over the three hundred feet cliffs; behind their heads was a tangled mass of thorn, stinging tree and burning vine, which the jungle always uses as a first line of defence; over in the coarse tussocks beyond the camp fire lived a large community of tiger snakes and death adders, which for centuries had been lords of this one, sun-baked ledge on the vast, gloomy plateau. Such trifles do not trouble men who carry a horse's pack all day, and so, undisturbed by the howling of dingoes and the scream of Powerful Owls, the first night passed in heavy sleep.[6]

Australia is a hard country and the people have had to adopt a starkly realistic view of life, or go under. In the bush, they usually go under anyway. One way to cope with a hard country and a tough life is through humour. Australian humour – realistic and sardonic – is used as a self-protective device to keep one's courage up in the face of inevitable disaster. This black humour involves an ironic acceptance of the fact that in the end, we all lose. Confronted by tanks, a digger said to his mate: 'You go that way and I'll go this way, and we'll surround 'em'. Deeply rooted in disjunctions – English versus Irish, male versus female, bush versus city, optimism versus pessimism – irony dominates Australian humour. Casual, shoulder-shrugging resignation leads to the stark conclusion that 'we can't win, no matter what' – the swagman in *Waltzing Matilda* died, the bushrangers Ned Kelly and Ben Hall perished, and many soldiers died pointlessly in the disaster at Gallipoli. Despite this, Australians continue to protest vigorously, and their vehicle for protest is swearing. Ned Kelly's description of the Victorian police is legendary:

> The brutal and cowardly conduct of big ugly fat-necked wombat-headed big-bellied magpie-legged narrow-hipped splay-footed sons of Irish Bailiffs or English landlords which is better known as officers of Justice or Victorian police.[7]

Laconic and stoical, Australians combine a calm acceptance of the fates with a grim humour. There is an old story about Percy Lindsay, having a drink with a few professional friends. The barmaid approached, apologised and asked the 'boys' if they would mind making less noise because her father had hanged himself in the back shed. After considering this for the time it took to finish their beer, they trooped out to the shed where Percy said: 'And sure enough there was the poor bastard hanging from a rafter dead as a doornail. He had his mouth half open in a funny way and looked a bit grim. We had quite a job getting him down'.

Such is life. The contrast with European angst, English class consciousness and American histrionics is obvious and makes this a very Australian story, even down to the words used in its telling. The barmaid says 'sorry' – a favourite Australian word used to inform unfortunate commuters that buses are out of service. Visitors note with amusement that Australians apologise for things that aren't their fault. 'Would you mind' is used obsessively to avoid the appearance of authoritarian behaviour, while 'a bit' is a popular expression used to qualify, if not further apologise for, the request. Visitors have also noted the irritating tendency of Australians, especially females, to end their sentences with rising intonation as if asking a question. 'We had a lovely holiday?' means 'We had a lovely holiday. Is that all right with you?' In Australia one must never place oneself above others.

Although European romanticism was an important influence on nineteenth-century writers, Irish romanticism was even more influential. In *The Irish in Australia*, Patrick O'Farrell argued that it is not the conflict between individual and the bush, but culture conflict (notably between the English and Irish) which explains the development of Australian society. The refusal of the Irish to act out a deferential role discomforted the English elite, eroded their feelings of superiority and announced that the old-world social order could not be reproduced in Australia. This produced a general atmosphere in which rigid hierarchies became increasingly difficult to sustain. It was the Irish and their friends who freed the atmosphere of authoritarianism, pretence and pomposity. The main unifying theme of Australian history is, for O'Farrell, the clash between the English majority (moderate, respectable, conformist), the Irish minority (melancholic, humorous, romantic, contradictory, volatile), and a local Australian minority (masculine, hedonist, non-intellectual).

The English thought that Australia should be a little England of the South Seas but the Irish minority promoted an Australian nationalism which repudiated the class-consciousness and conservatism of British society. The Irish were enemies of pretentiousness, pomposity and repression, indifferent to worldly progress, and friends of innocent merriment, mischief and passionate tragedy. O'Farrell notes that while the non-Irish rich and powerful built commercial and industrial empires, the Irish preferred anonymity, equality, and the security of their own kind as their vision of a good life. It was a vote for the underdog, but its danger lay in glorifying the role of underdog with his fatalism, his suspicion of excellence, and his sense of grievance.

Yet it would be a gross oversimplification to suggest that early Australians did not value skill and effectiveness. Nor is it true that they were opposed to authority in all its forms. While Australians oppose authoritarians on principle, they are relatively accepting of authoritative individuals or experts. This is well demonstrated in the case of the Australian fighting soldiers in the First World War.

Known collectively as the Australian Imperial Force, it was created from nothing: no history, no elite regiments and no martial tradition. But the diggers created a tradition of their own: unsurpassed courage in fighting; indiscipline on the parade ground; riotous behaviour on rest and recreation leave; constant swearing; heavy drinking; fiercely independent and opportunistic behaviour; and masterful use of irony and sardonic humour. Away from the battlefield their discipline was lax to the point of anarchic.

General William Birdwood dined out many times on the following story of his inspection of an Australian camp. Leaning against a gate was a sentry, gun yards away, who showed no interest in the general with a plumed hat. He neither moved nor saluted. The general was furious. Briskly he marched up to the sentry.

'Soldier', he said, 'You didn't salute me'.

'That's right', agreed the sentry.

'Why not?' demanded the general. The soldier shrugged away the absurdity of such a question.

'Do you know who I *am*?' asked an increasingly furious British general.

The soldier surveyed him from his shining boots to the feathered plume in his hat.

'No idea,' he answered.

'I'm General Birdwood, your commander-in-chief', the furious officer told him.

'Well, in that case,' replied the soldier flatly, 'why don't you shove your feathers up your arse and fly away, like any other bird would'.[8]

In *The Myth of the Digger*, Jane Ross argues that the diggers recognised the general legitimacy of the army system (as they did bureaucracies generally). But in granting legitimacy to each officer his formal role was of relatively little importance. Legitimacy was granted on a limited and revocable basis. If an officer proved incompetent or did not care for his men, his influence was severely circumscribed. This didn't matter much to the diggers, since they had no need of leaders anyway. Ross argued that these restrictions on the granting of legitimacy should not be construed to mean that the diggers were 'anti- authority'. The diggers believed they were entitled to receive reasons to support the orders they were expected to carry out. And it was reasons they demanded and received. For the diggers, the legitimacy of a power relationship depended on the personal qualities of the officer rather than on his formal claims to power as a holder of a commission. While the diggers were not generally hostile to officers, they were irritated by those who claimed more than their due in respect of privileges, or who gained commissions for the wrong reasons. They reserved the right to rely on their judgement, expected officers to be fair and to issue orders in a particular way. Australian officers had high standards set for them by subordinates who were more critical of those who wielded power than were their colleagues in more deferential armies. But what did the diggers require of their officers?

Australians expected not only military skills from their officers, but also courage and common sense. If the officers didn't measure up, they should be sent back to base. Believing that fighting was a straightforward task which most Australians could undertake with little effort, the diggers resisted training. If almost anyone can fight, there was no need to defer to officers since any fighting man could be an officer. An officer was obeyed if he explained why his orders should be followed. If diggers were satisfied that the orders given by the officer were necessary and accorded with common sense, they carried them out with vigour and courage. If the orders made no sense to them, the officer had a problem. If the digger was given an order he wanted to know what it was all about. If he was satisfied that it was necessary and that it was common sense he would carry out that order through all the fires of hell.

While the battlefield abounded with good officers, the base camps had the worst bureaucratic characteristics. Camp officers were obese, lazy, incompetent soldiers who were obsessed with army rituals and regulations. The diggers called them captains of flatulence and treated them with disdain. According to Jane Ross, they were 'broken dolls' and 'staff drones' who lacked courage, initiative, decisiveness, independence, irreverence and common sense. In short, fighting was valued far more highly than administrative skills. Bureaucrats have never had an easy time of it in Australia.

Australians have long understood the inadequacies of action, even though they enjoy action. They know how to be heroes without a cause and strive to suffer ordeals sardonically. Dogmatic pronouncements about Australians being anti-authority are, therefore, unwarranted and probably derive from confusing power with authority. Australians recognise the value of authority when they want to know why they should do what is asked of them. Their language might have been mutinous but they dismissed mutineers contemptuously as 'fucking no-hopers', 'fellers who ought to have their heads read', 'bloody fools who had gone completely off their rockers'. As Jane Ross noted, they were rebels against hierarchy but obeyed orders if it was reasonable to do so.

According to historian W.K. Hancock in his 1930 book, *Australia*, the locals are not content merely to attack privilege or social status. Rather, they are inclined to ignore capacities in their preoccupation with needs. Australian democracy favours equality of enjoyment over equality of opportunity. Hancock argues that Australian democracy has done much to equalise opportunities, but it has also done something to narrow them. Australians are anxious that everybody should run a fair race. But they are resentful if anybody runs a fast race. Indeed, they dislike altogether the idea of a race, because in a race, victory is to the strong. Their sympathy is for the underdog, and their will is to make merit take a place in the queue.

While they are supposed to be matter-of-fact folk who distrust politicians and their rhetoric, Australians have been incurably romantic in their faith in the power of government to fulfil their needs. They have been too prepared to water good wine so that there may be enough for everybody, even though many males prefer beer.

Hancock saw in this volatile mixture of romantic sentiments a challenge for Australians to create their own values and sweep away the old quarrels of the day before yesterday. If the values of the old world were to be rejected, new values would be needed. It is unsurprising, therefore, that several artists of a century ago were attracted to the philosophy of Nietzsche, who called for a revaluation of all values. But by the 1930s, Australians had compromised their romantic idealism and settled for everything that Nietzsche loathed – a 'middling standard'. Nietzsche proved too demanding, too aristocratic and too contemptuous of the average Australian.

The fierce nationalism promoted by the 'bohemians of the *Bulletin*' in Sydney expressed itself as a vindication of equality and democracy and an assertion of the supreme worth of the common man. Such a philosophy is hardly Nietzschean.

Democratic nationalism reinforced with Henry Lawson's gospel of mateship and the romanticising of the bushman by the *Bulletin* school of writers, produced the legendary Australian ambivalence to authority.

Australian attitudes to authority are paradoxical: the quest for equality has been satisfied to a large extent by the establishment of bureaucratic institutions. During the colonial era, each of the six colonies developed a complex system for dealing with domestic problems, while the British government retained responsibility for defence, external relations and other central government functions. These were transferred to the Commonwealth government at federation, but the states retained many of the most important powers, including taxation, until the Second World War. These peculiar historical circumstances have resulted in the complaint that Australia is one of the most over-governed countries in the world, with many functions duplicated at state, federal and local government levels. Australians believe that government exists to service individual rights so that the state should be a vast public utility devoted to providing happiness for the greatest possible number of citizens. Accordingly, Australians have developed a talent for bureaucracy. In the city and the country, where individualism is strong, bureaucratic behaviour is deeply ingrained. Understandably, Australians take a dubious pride in this since it appears to contradict the cherished image of antiauthoritarian, ungovernable individualists. Where is the rugged individualist who scorns authority? With many public servants to take care of their needs, Australians sacrificed rugged individualism for a gospel of relaxation.

In his aptly named book, *Land of the Long Weekend*, Ronald Conway describes Australia in the 1970s as the country where weekdays are days of R&R which help the locals recover from the last weekend and prepare for the next weekend. Symptomatic of the late twentieth-century Australian lifestyle was an obsessive dedication to immature consumerism, mortgaged luxury, brick-veneered suburbia and unearned leisure. As a result of the breakdown of family relationships, Australians turned to a peer-group lifestyle based on superficial and unconvincing mateship. Australia is one of the highest-ranking Western countries in terms of the number of holidays and its administrators have cunningly contrived to have most of them occur on a Monday. The long weekend has thus become a national symbol in a country where pleasure is linked with novelty and 'getting away from it all'. But what are they getting away from? Surely not a life of hard work since, as every Australian knows, the innumerable underperformers are not confined to blue-collar workers involved in heavy manual labour, but include employees at all levels of work organisations. Australians have always been plagued by vagueness, tardiness, incompetence and vacuous unconcern from public servants and members of the (misnamed) service industry. While it is easy and tempting to attribute this widespread apathy and incompetence to the values of Australian workers, it is positively impious to blame workers for their shortcomings. And the same applies to managers who one might have thought play an important role in ensuring that their colleagues perform effectively. Yet managers have indirectly encouraged incompetence in their colleagues for fear that direct confrontation will not be worth the effort.

The workplace is not a place for work: it is a place to prepare for and recover from the far more stimulating activities of the weekend, especially those concerned with sport.

The national obsession with sport carries with it an affirmation of human courage and endurance where physical achievement is the standard by which individuals are assessed. The obsession with sport, however, seems to contradict Australia's notorious 'levelling tendency': a mistrust of excellence and suspicion of celebrities. As everybody knows, Australians have a decidedly ambivalent, if not negative, attitude toward individual eminence and distinction, with the exception of sport. Australians often qualify their comments about leadership with, 'except in sport', although that expression is generally further qualified with 'so long as they are good blokes': unpretentious, modest, laconic in victory. They should not appear 'uppity', arrogant or self-assertive and they should not indulge in American-style self-glorification.

A major weakness of folk history is that commentators abstract popular values from the local literature and apply them to the general population. Are our profound and lovable values – egalitarianism, mateship, tolerance, friendliness, stoicism and sardonic humour – characteristic of suburban Australians?

In *Intruders in the Bush*, John Carroll argues that there have been three main influences on Australian culture: upper-middle class Victorian values and institutions; working class (especially Irish) egalitarianism; and twentieth-century consumerism. Middle-class Australians settled themselves into British-style suburbs dominated by British-style houses and sent their children to British-style schools where they played cricket and rugby. However, in the late nineteenth century, working-class Irish-Australians staged a cultural take-over of English values. At its heart was an egalitarian ethos with an accompanying intolerance of respectability and manners, hostility to formal authority, a talent for improvisation but also for bureaucracy, and a romantic attitude toward male comradeship.

Carroll argued that the only thing that is typically Australian about the egalitarian-mateship phenomenon is that it is more widespread than in other Western countries. This ethic has been prominent in Australia because of the peculiar nature and strength of the working-class experience, and the fact that the upper-middle class, including senior managers as a class, has not been able to enshrine its values. This failure was due not to lack of strength but to lack of confidence. The values and manners of this class have remained the preserve of a small minority.

Why did the middle class fail to consolidate its culture? Carroll's thesis is that the formation of Australian society coincided with a general development in the West whereby the middle class came progressively under the influence of an egalitarian bad conscience. He argued that democracies suppress excellence and individuality and encourage disdain for hierarchy, which makes it inevitable that central governments increase their power. But above all, the egalitarian spirit of democracies legitimates the envy of difference and of superiority. So the targets of envy establish disarming strategies by disguising whatever is likely to be coveted. This fear of envy is a contributing factor to the bad conscience of the modern middle class. The pressure to maintain disarming strategies may result in a questioning of the very values once so vigorously defended. The Puritan virtues of hard work, frugal living and responsibility for community require committed belief and action. Living in a country lacking in tradition and born of cultural conflict, Australians do not believe deeply enough, or in sufficient numbers, in these values. Where the authority of an old culture collapses there is a strong tendency for people to identify with the victims. This is what happened in Australia and accounts for its citizens' empathy with underdogs, the lower classes, the stressed, the deviant and criminal. Carroll noted that this middle-class bad conscience is not new to post-1950 Australia since it was well established in the myth-makers of the 1890s who were significantly urban middle class.

Over the past thirty-five years, Australian characteristics have been changed by feminism, multiculturalism and postmodernism. The traditional 'true blue' stereotype is acknowledged by a small minority and less than fifteen percent of Australians identify with the man on the land. The majority do not identify with this easy-going, down-to-earth, masculine, anti-intellectual Australian. By contrast, many see themselves as sophisticated, ambitious, hard-working, generous, creative, egalitarian, loyal and tolerant. As a consequence of the increasing feminisation of life in Australia, males have become more willing to express their feelings. One has only to watch popular television programs to see men crying when confronted with a newly improved backyard. However, Australians have also become passive, soft, simplistic, materialistic and obese. They demand that their politicians and bureaucrats work for them, but are cynical about their ability to do so.

If Australians rely so heavily on bureaucracy one might expect them to value leadership. However, their cynical attitude to politicians, bureaucrats and managers militates against leadership, at least from them. So Australians live an exasperating paradox: paradoxical because they depend on politicians, bureaucrats and managers but don't trust them; exasperating because they pursue a goal that is doomed to failure. Believing that Australian democracy could, as Henry Lawson said, 'democratise the world', they are exasperated by the failure of government and business to eliminate hierarchies of power, corruption and inefficiencies. Their exasperation is expressed through strident demands for politicians and managers to work more effectively for the people, even though they know they will not. The result is a constant discrediting of politicians, public servants and managers.

There have been no leaders in the country's history who have been able to seduce the Australian people for long, or at all. Australians have managed to combine a conditional egalitarianism with a strong sense of their independence and this has been achieved by a strong belief in universalism in law and an associated sense of fair play and support for the underdog. These assertions need to be qualified somewhat, but for now the point can be made that Australians are wary of those in positions of power. This is the most positive aspect of the Australian Tall-Poppy Syndrome, since it has prevented the emergence of leaders, or at least ensured that their status is temporary.

The Tall-Poppy phenomenon is alive and well in Australia in the twenty-first century. For her book *Local Heroes*, Ann-Maree Moodie interviewed thirty-seven influential men and women – entrepreneurs, politicians, scientists, artists, architects, writers, business executives, journalists and athletes. All but three agreed that the Tall-Poppy Syndrome exists in Australia.

No one has captured the Australian character better than Les Murray.[9] Combining a reference to the vast open spaces and the local laconic style, Murray sees sprawl as the quality of the farmer who cut down his Rolls-Royce into a truck, and sprawl is what the company lacked when it tried to retrieve the car to repair its image. Sprawl cannot be dressed for, not even in running shoes worn with mink and a nose ring. That's Society or Style. Sprawl is more like the thirteenth banana in a dozen. Sprawl is an image of Australia and would that it were more so. Reprimanded and dismissed, it listens with a grin and a boot up on the rail of possibility. It may have to leave the earth. But it scratches the other cheek and thinks it unlikely.

2

MANAGERS AND MATES

Laconic: Management style that makes inarticulateness a virtue.

Readers may well object that this romantic indulgence in literature is anachronistic and irrelevant to the current concerns of Australians, especially those in the business of management. After all, these philosophical speculations were products of the romantic fantasies of urban intellectuals, not a few of whom were overly addicted to alcohol. Most Australians know little of the bush and care not a wink about its existential implications. They are suburbanites who rarely venture more than a hundred kilometres from the security of home base, except for tropical holidays. Is it not therefore fanciful and misleading to burden Australians with tensions and agonies that simply do not apply to most of them? A suburban existence dominated by the cretinising effects of the mass and social media protects individuals from existential angst to such an extent that Australians can happily claim that 'we are all individuals'. Of course, it is possible, and some think likely, that the characteristic behaviour of Australians is a smoke-screen for their inability to make the dynamic adjustments of which Americans are proud. The laconic Australian way is, on this view, little more than a pathetic attempt to ward off the presence of those who have developed consummate social skills which threaten artless folk. To go further, to suggest that Australians disvalue performance might suggest that they have yet to find themselves. Their hollowness, so often commented upon by Asian and European visitors, may be a sad fact. Is their disdain for politicians, bureaucrats and managers a well-rehearsed cynical romanticism? Or is it mere adolescent rebellion?

Distrusting managers, Australians nonetheless demand much of them and grudgingly respect those who demonstrate such personal qualities as tough-minded realism, initiative, courage or sardonic humour. Since there are few opportunities to demonstrate these qualities in their jobs, managers are ridiculed rather than respected. The only people who believe that managers are leaders are managers, and some of them are not sure.

Australian managers have never enjoyed a good reputation, even within their own ranks. Only at two activities are Australians incurably mediocre – government and business. So wrote Hugh Stretton, echoing Donald Horne, who lamented the fact that it is Australians' misfortune that their affairs are controlled by second-rate men – 'racketeers of the mediocre who have risen to authority in a non-competitive community where they are protected in their adaptations of other people's ideas'.[1] Yet there are, according to Stretton, grounds for hope in our 'profound and lovable virtues': a friendly, not-too-competitive society that is still the world's most egalitarian in manners, if not in fact.[2] The problem for Australians is how to combine our profound and lovable virtues with the pragmatic demands of management.

Australian managers complain bitterly about excessive government control of their business lives. Yet, when companies run into trouble they want the government to solve their problems for them. Sadly, many government bureaucrats have been only too willing to comply, thus supporting capitalism for workers and socialism for over-paid managers. Obscene levels of executive remuneration, even for rank incompetents, have led to increasing cynicism about the quality and worth of managers, even within their own ranks.

Australian managers have been widely portrayed as artless, unsophisticated and transparent. Not for them the ruthless confrontation supported by devious strategies to achieve personal goals. Rather, they are an engaging mix of humanity, consideration and conformity. Whereas Americans are performance-orientated, Australian managers suffer certain doubts. If performance is everything, one has to applaud and reward outstanding performers irrespective of their behaviour. And this Australians will not do. If it is true that the English expect to lose at sport with dignity and Americans to win without it, then Australians aim for performance with caveats. Since Australian managers are determined quietly to defend their quality of life, they have been sceptical about imported management ideas and practices, and those that appear to threaten quality of life are allowed quietly to wither on the vine. Direct confrontation with overseas experts and gurus is not the Australian way. Rather, the gurus' seminars are well attended, their jargon briefly adopted, lucrative commissions concluded, but the 'new' management models are rarely applied.

One difficulty in trying to understand Australian managers is that, given local values, they are regarded as mediocre by definition. Of course it is possible that Australian managers are mediocre in fact and deserve their reputation as 'racketeers of the mediocre'. Reading between the lines of government reports and academic articles, it appears that their reputation for mediocrity is based on international comparisons with American managers. Are Australian managers regarded as mediocre because they oppose the profound and lovable virtues of American pragmatism?

Australian managers face a daunting task if they are regarded as mediocre by definition. Indeed, it is difficult to imagine what it would take for Australian managers to be widely respected and even revered. They are faced, therefore, with an apparently insoluble problem: trying to promote local values, they manage not to manage. Realising that 'getting on with colleagues' is important to their survival, they have danced around American-style confrontation, preferring a unique form of humanism which emphasises performance *and* personality, management *and* psychology. For many years, Australian managers have danced with psychologists. And Australia has produced several eminent dancing partners.

Julie Marshall and Richard Trahair published *Industrial Psychology in Australia to 1950*. 332 of the 1551 articles in the book are devoted to incentive schemes and profit-sharing. By comparison, there were only 169 articles on personnel management, industrial psychology (including counselling and mental health) and 88 articles on management training, education, management traits and attitudes.

In 1911, 13 articles appeared in *The Argus* and *Australasian Manufacturer* about profit-sharing and schemes which allow employees to become shareholders of companies. This interest culminated in a request in 1914 by the Liberal Workers' Institute to ask the Minister for Home Affairs to provide statistics with a view to introducing such schemes in Australia. Profit-sharing, industrial co-partnership, industrial fatigue and the Taylor system of scientific management were the dominant subjects during the war. By 1917 the NSW Railway Commissioner was attacked publicly for criticising scientific management. After the war, discussion of interviewing, selecting and vocational training marked a shift towards the personnel function.

Bernard Muscio delivered a series of influential lectures at the University of Sydney on occupational selection, scientific management and work fatigue. In 1920 he published *Lectures in Industrial Administration,* in which he argued that industrial psychology should concentrate on the study of 'mental' factors and the selection of workers to achieve the best results from work. In 1924 there was light relief when an American 'characterologist' lectured on his method of employee selection, claiming that he studied character from the proportionate developments of the brain, face and body from which he predicted occupational success.

The most famous Australian in the history of management, (George) Elton Mayo, emphasised the social and emotional factors which influence workplace behaviour. In 1929, he was appointed professor of industrial research at the Harvard School of Business Administration and through the Department of Industrial Research there, participated in the Hawthorne studies at Western Electric's Chicago plant. He enjoyed an academic career of almost thirty years and was widely honoured in his native land at the time of his death.

In 1927 the NSW Chamber of Manufactures established the Australian Institute of Industrial Psychology, which actively promoted psychological research. H. Tasman Lovell published papers on the 'psychology of salesmanship' and at the University of Sydney, A.H. Martin, arguably the father of Australian personnel management, taught courses in industrial psychology to managers. In 1931 the Australian Institute of Industrial Psychology published his *Three Lectures in Industrial Psychology*. After wittily dismissing such pseudo-sciences as astrology, palmistry, physiognomy, phrenology and graphology, he enthusiastically supported the development of vocational tests in industry. In discussing the desirable qualities for successful salesmen, he emphasised dress and deportment, voice, general aptitude and intelligence, personality qualities – extraversion, humour, resilience, diplomacy and self-confidence.

After the Second World War psychologists promoted themselves vigorously. In 1949 the director of the Australian Institute of Industrial Psychology published an article in *Rydges* called 'Psychology – Management's Ally', which focused on selection and vocational guidance. R.J. Chambers described the first Australian management diploma course offered by the Industrial Management Department of the Sydney Technical

College. To the surprise of many, the course included subjects in general and social psychology.[3]

Also in 1949 Tom Pauling co-authored an influential article for *Public Administration* about personnel management in the NSW Public Service which argued for the increasing importance of the personnel manager.[4] A one-time Australian rugby international, Pauling became one of Sydney's best-known personnel managers at Bradmill and Philips where he pioneered, with psychologist Evan Davies, the use of personality tests in industry. I had the good fortune to study industrial psychology with Evan Davies at the University of NSW and worked with Tom Pauling at Philips in the late 1960s. On presenting me with a copy of Herzberg's best-seller, Pauling noted that 'he got it half-right'. Typically, he did not tell me which half was right.

By the 1940s, surveys revealed that fifty-five percent of firms had personnel departments. Personnel developed a more professional character with the development of tertiary training in personnel administration and the establishment of professional associations, such as the Institute of Industrial Management (later the Australian Institute of Management) and the Institute of Personnel Management (Australia).

After 1950 a trend in industrial psychology made significant inroads into Australian management through personnel departments. Crusaders of this trend were the 'human relations' experts who built their case for psychology on the American Hawthorne experiments. They argued for social motivators and against economic motivators. Although the majority of managers had assumed that money was the greatest incentive for employees, American psychologists insisted that employees needed other, less tangible rewards. Because of the confusion generated by the debate about motivation and the role of money as an incentive, researchers increased their efforts to understand the relationship between job satisfaction and performance. They concluded that satisfaction with one's job is not necessarily related to performance and job performance may be only peripherally related to personal goals. We don't know what the majority of managers thought about this debate since there are no major studies of Australian business managers before the 1960s.

Sociologist Sol Encel, in *Equality and Authority*, reported a survey from 1960 of 100 senior managers which portrayed them as lacking in community leadership, political knowledge, aspirations and achievements. He acknowledged politician and author Michael Baume, who described business (in 1964) as the most poorly serviced vocation in Australia, made up from the leftovers of other professions. Australia's prosperity, he argued, depends on good luck rather than on any inspired managerial activity. Business directors are created out of the remnants after medicine, law, science and engineering have taken the better intellects. A worrying feature of Australian managers was their anti-intellectualism and hostility towards tertiary education. Even today one hears echoes of Henry Ford's boorish attitude towards education (history is bunk), as managers rationalise their intellectual inferiority complexes with displays of bravado when confronted by articulate and erudite colleagues. Many Australian managers simply lack confidence in their ability to converse intelligently with others; retreating behind a facile pragmatism which sneers at education and promotes dubious forms of training based on the learning of routine skills or jejune models of 'managerial style'.

In the early years of Australian management, neither training nor education was required. Unlike members of the traditional professions, managers could scarcely believe their good fortunes when they secured well-paid jobs without formal education. Prior to the 1970s when management schools opened their doors, Australian managers were notoriously practical folk who were wary of, if not antagonistic towards, intellectual pursuits. They defended practice against theory, experience against intellect and training against education. This anti-intellectualism, which is characteristic of Australian life generally, is unsurprising given the difficulty in agreeing on a curriculum for management studies. People who have justified their occupational existence (and high salaries) on their ability to survive a succession of bureaucratic jobs are unlikely to agree on a management curriculum. Indeed, one of the more tedious assertions of Australian managers over the years has been their insistence that they achieved success without formal education.

The days of uneducated managers were numbered, however. Late in 1969 the Commonwealth Government commissioned an 'Inquiry into Postgraduate Education for Management'. The report of that inquiry, known as the *Cyert Report*, was completed in four weeks and tabled in March 1970. The members of the Committee of Inquiry were American academics who recommended the creation of a 'school of excellence' in postgraduate management education at the University of NSW, thus upsetting the Melbourne business establishment. A second (Ralph) Committee of Inquiry into management education was commissioned in 1980 and Melbourne got its 'school of excellence'.

By 1970, five Australian universities offered MBA-type programs – Adelaide, Macquarie, Melbourne, Monash and New South Wales. After a slow start, the programs eventually numbered among the economic success stories of tertiary education. Some academics, however, expressed grave doubts and considerable disquiet about the existence of management schools in universities. They were concerned that management schools would be unable to maintain academic standards since new courses had to be invented and old ones modified for business consumption. This was forced upon management teachers by the demands of pragmatic, ill-educated managers, increasingly illiterate students and the urgent need to establish lines of professional demarcation. The fact that academics could not agree on the status of management added to the confusion: is it a science, an art, or a practice?

As management is an interdisciplinary subject its academic founders took the liberal position that its study should include 'hard' subjects, like statistics and 'soft' subjects, like psychology. These were supplemented with functional courses in finance, marketing and logistics. Of special importance were 'people' courses, which have travelled under many names – organisational behaviour, industrial/organisational/managerial psychology – and since the 1980s, human resource management. The 'people' courses directed attention to the personalities, motives and values of managers.

In the late 1960s Geert Hofstede, in *Culture's Consequences*, studied the values of 116,000 IBM employees in forty countries. He found Australians to be strongly individualistic, masculine, with low levels of anxiety (uncertainty avoidance). Strong individualism means that: the involvement of individuals with their organisations is calculative rather than moralistic; organisations are not expected to look after their employees for life; organisations have only a moderate influence on members' well-being; employees are expected to defend their own interests rather than allow management to represent them; and policies and practices allow for individual initiative rather than emphasising loyalty to employers. Strong masculinity means that: organisational interests are a legitimate reason for interfering with people's private lives; fewer females are in the more qualified jobs; females in the more qualified jobs are very assertive; higher job stress; and more industrial conflict.

Hofstede's results indicated that Australians adopt a self-interested attitude about work, are easy-going in their attitudes towards work rules, but give little support to reforms that would require more involvement by employees in decision-making. In short, Australians are generally willing to allow managers to exercise authority in return for economic security.

In their 1974 book, *The Australian Manager*, Byrt and Masters describe the ideal manager as a person who formulates and implements strategy, makes decisions, organises people and carries out professional, technical or operative work. They insist that management is not a profession, in the way in which the law and medicine are professions and argue that Australian managers do not form a political class. They describe Australian (middle) managers as:

> Dependent on government; insular; lacking in boldness and initiative; dependent on overseas sources for capital, ideas and techniques; reasonably but not highly educated; masculine in fact and outlook; city-dwellers, in particular of either Sydney or Melbourne; conservative; fearful of radicalism in economics and politics; egalitarian both socially and at the work place; practical and pragmatic; opportunists rather than planners; non-intellectual and some are anti-intellectual; interested in leisure, social activity and family; critical of politicians and the holders of formal authority; versatile; materialist; non-aggressive; manipulative in managerial style; and low in Machiavellian characteristics.[5]

In the second (1982) edition of their book, these descriptions do not appear and no explanation is offered. Clearly, their descriptions of local managers in the first edition were not flattering and did not correspond to the 'ideal' manager found in American management books.

In 1996 I asked more than 1000 managers to rate themselves as a group according to Byrt's and Masters' descriptions. They agreed with them on all counts: the impressionistic ratings of managers by two academics from the University of Melbourne in the early 1970s were almost identical to managers' ratings more than twenty years later.

In the mid-1970s, an American named G.W. England compared Australian managers with their counterparts in the U.S., India, South Korea and Japan. In *The Manager and His Values*, England argues that personal value systems of managers do not change rapidly, even during periods of significant social change. The Australian managers in his study were humanistic and placed a low value on conflict, profit, growth, competition, risk, success, achievement and leadership. Overall, the Australians revealed a strong degree of humanistic idealism and, therefore, a relatively low degree of pragmatism in their decision-making. England asks whether it is possible to combine (Australian) humanism, with its emphasis on tolerance, security and getting on with each other, with (American) values based on high achievement, competence, profit maximisation and organisational efficiency. We might conclude that it is difficult. American managers valued organisational efficiency whereas Australians valued employee welfare and humane bureaucracy. England argues that Australians' attitudes towards tolerance, compassion, trust, loyalty, honour, employee and social welfare suggest that they are more embracing of organisational egalitarianism than American managers who vehemently reject the idea.

George Renwick wrote a report for Esso Eastern Inc. on differences between Australians and Americans.[6] He begins by pointing to the similarities: the two countries are frontier societies founded by immigrants from the British Isles whose origins are Anglo-Celtic and whose social values are individualistic and democratic. Both peoples are sociable, informal, forthright, practical, inventive, and non, or even anti-intellectual. Relationships between them should, therefore, be mutually satisfying. But they are not. Confusion and conflict often arise. After trying to work together, Americans often feel that Australians are cynical and undisciplined. Australians, for their part, feel that Americans are superficial and pretentious. Where Americans have friends, Australians have mates. Australians respect and share loyalty to friends and expect deeper commitments than do Americans who place a high value on merely being friendly. Australians believe strongly that one supports one's mate no matter what. Americans are more conscious of sticking to their job and getting through their work. Americans need to be liked but laconic Australians do not tell them that they are liked. Wanting to be respected, Americans do things that they think will impress others and expect a favourable response. But it is very difficult to impress Australians, who are impatient with attempts to gain their favour. In conversation, Australians are cynical, especially when they correct American enthusiasm. Australians, especially men, believe that words should be used sparingly, or not at all. If they have to speak, they speak without expression to indicate that the subject is hardly worth talking about, except to 'get a rise' out of others. And so Australians use hundreds of colourful terms to convey a tone of amiable contempt. Critical of excessive ambition, boastfulness and pretentiousness, they resent any attempt to 'pull rank'. Accordingly, Americans see them as crude and critical. When asked about a person's performance or the quality of a product, Australians say, 'she'll be right'. When given orders from an American, their response is passive resistance. Americans believe that Australians consider work to be a nuisance and do as little of it as slowly as they can. Australians believe that work is a national joke and people who work hard are likely to attract suspicion. Americans believe that they can do anything if they work hard enough; Australians believe they can do anything but, unless it is an emergency, it isn't worth the effort.

In 1980 I published the results of a study comparing Australian managers' views on industrial relations over a period of twenty-three years.[7] In the mid-1950s, Kenneth Walker investigated managers' and trade unionists' attitudes to the sources of industrial conflict in Australia. Both groups tended to emphasise legal and economic factors. The later research showed that although economic issues remained important, the emphasis had shifted to psychological factors. Managers were inclined to attribute industrial conflict to greed, lack of cooperation and poor team spirit among their employees; union officials blamed the autocratic, selfish and uncooperative behaviour of managers. These findings points to the increasing 'psychologising' of workplace behaviour and the tendency to include personality as explanations of work performance. In this way conflict at work is attributed to particular personalities, or personality disorders, rather than to the relationships in which behaviour is embedded. The tendency to psychologise industrial conflict was strongest among senior managers and reflected a prevailing view that anyone with ability who is willing to work hard can get into senior management and that the difference between the highest and lowest incomes in Australia is neither excessive nor unfair. This view implies that those at the top fought a hard battle to get there and are qualified to tell those below what to do, and the system is fair because everyone has an equal chance to engage in the battle. Historically, Australian managers have used this argument to justify resistance to any dilution of their rights or prerogatives. Implicit in this ideology is approval of and support for the existing pattern of power relationships. In Walker's study the main factors making for industrial conflict were legal, economic and, in principle, changeable. However, as industrial problems are attributed to the personalities of managers, it becomes more difficult to take constructive steps toward solution. This produces two possible reactions. On the one hand, it gives weight to the radical argument that only extensive social change can reduce the level of conflict between managers and others. On the other hand, it encourages those with a more conservative bent to accept the status quo and emphasise the personalities involved in management relationships.

In *The Seven Cultures of Capitalism*, Charles Hampden-Turner and Fons Trompenaars studied managerial values from more than fifty countries. They found that Americans are the most strongly committed to Protestant Ethic values – universalism, analysis, individualism, inner-directedness and achievement. Managers from the historically Protestant countries – U.K., U.S., (British) Canada, (Northern) Germany, Holland, New Zealand and Australia – endorsed these values to a much greater degree than did managers from the Catholic countries of Western Europe and Asia. Like Americans, Australian managers are strongly committed to universalism, analysis, individualism, inner-directedness; but unlike Americans, Australians suffer certain doubts about the relative importance of achieved status. Americans are more likely than managers from other countries to believe that winning is what counts. But if winning is everything, nothing else matters. In Australia, however, other things do matter: how one copes with success matters.

I had the pleasure of working in Germany with Fons Trompenaars on a course for senior Western European managers. We asked them to nominate the dominant management model (or metaphor) for several countries. There was almost unanimous agreement that the dominant management models were: U.S. – the football team; England – the class system; Germany – the machine; Asia – the family; and Australia – the barbecue.

It is clear that studies of Australian management values over a period of nearly fifty years reveal a surprising consistency in their conclusions. Australian managers endorse a form of home-grown humanism which tries to harmonise work performance with quality of life generally. England's study is important since it is the first to emphasise Australian managers' commitment to an ideology of humanism. The study from Hampden-Turner and Trompenaars is important because it suggests that, while Australian managers are similar to Americans in their support for broadly-based Protestant values, their humanism acts as a brake on their commitment to performance.

The 1990s were not good years for the reputation of Australian managers. The OECD in its 1992 *World*

Competitiveness Report rated Australian managers as 'ineffectual', ranking them nineteenth out of twenty-two member countries. The *Leadership Report* undertaken by Monash University found Australian managers to be egalitarian, responsive, forthright, but indecisive and risk averse. Then along came the *Karpin Report*, which was three years in the making and a waste of $6 million of taxpayers' money. Formally known as the *Industry Task Force on Leadership and Management Skills*, it was established in 1992 and advertised as the most comprehensive study of Australian managers ever undertaken. That it was, but it was also dominated by management consultants, confused definitions, inadequate methodologies and management jargon. And it offered no new ideas.

In February 1995 the report of the Task Force appeared under the politically correct title of *Enterprising Nation: Renewing Australia's Managers to Meet the Challenges of the Asia-Pacific Century* – and was predictably critical of Australian managers and management education. The main conclusion was that Australian managers are hard-working, flexible, technically sound, egalitarian, open, genuine, honest and ethical. But they are also poor at team work and empowerment, unable to cope with change and lacking in people skills. The egalitarian nature of Australian managers was considered a weakness because it had an adverse effect on decision-making and resulted in managers' reluctance to confront subordinates with issues of poor performance. The authors concluded that while the best Australian managers are the equal of the best in the world, there are very few of them. Furthermore, Australian managers are perceived internationally as considerably inferior to Japanese, American, British and German managers. Even among their colleagues, Australian managers were judged to be well below acceptable international standards.

Releasing *Enterprising Nation* to the public in April 1995, David Karpin suggested that Australians need to revere their business leaders. He made the familiar pleas for more women in management, best-practice management – Australians should be more like American managers – and more and better training and education. But the bad news was that there were no 'world-class management schools' in Australia. We need management schools that employ around 110 academics and our little schools are well below that number. Therefore, we are not world-class schools.

Newspaper headlines were predictable: 'Australians: No Brains for Business' (*Australian Financial Review*); 'Report Slams Managers' (*Courier Mail*); and 'Schools Not up to World Standard' (*The Australian*). With a few exceptions, Australian journalists delighted in reporting our faults to the world.

Writing in the *Sydney Morning Herald*, Gerard Henderson thought it appropriate that the *Karpin Report* was launched on the day after Anzac Day: another Aussie failure. He concluded that there was not much enterprise in the *Karpin Report* and pointed to its bland observations. He acknowledged that the authors asked important questions but their recommendations were pedestrian and bureaucratic. The Report abounds with clichés and tautologies:

'All enterprises are experiencing change as we move towards the twenty-first century'. Well, fancy that. Finally, the authors' indulgence in simplistic theory is embarrassing. For example, we are supposed to believe that we are moving from old to new 'paradigms of management'. Once upon a time managers were consumed by 'vicious circles' but now they are blessed with 'virtuous circles'. 'The essential problem with *Enterprising Nation* is that it bagged Australian managers without defining precisely whom it had in mind...As a short, middle-aged Anglo-Celt, I keep my weighty volumes to stand on as required.[8]

Fred Emery thought that the *Karpin Report* was a 'deeply disappointing blockbuster'. He criticised the authors for assuming that management is a newly emergent science. Management is not and never will be a science, yet the authors assumed that there is an emerging body of empirically-grounded knowledge that is worthy of the title 'management sciences' which are applicable to anything called management. More importantly, Emery wondered why the authors of the Report did not ask whether changes in the workforce towards self-managing groups eliminate the need for the supervisors who are included in the authors' definition of 'manager'. They assumed that supervisors can be retrained as leaders, mentors and coaches. This is assumed in the face of one fact, which they probably did not know, that in the 1950s the movement to retrain supervisors in human relations was a dismal failure; and in the face of another fact, which they certainly did know, that human resource people do not know how to train the much better-schooled managers to be leaders, mentors and coaches.

The analysis of the task-force reveals that Australian management is faced with more of the same old challenges; the recommendations add up to more of the same old solutions. Although the Report lists a depressingly long series of complaints about the state and insularity of Australian management education, it can do no more than recommend higher salaries for professors, forming one really big national school of management and capping the lot with a national body to certify management education and "continue the work of the task force". Heaven forbid.[9]

If it is true that Australian managers are criticised for being insufficiently American, it does not follow that they should replace Australian humanism (which defines truth as correspondence with the facts) with American pragmatism (which defines truth as what works). If truth is what works for different groups, the dominant group's 'truth' will quickly become the received wisdom until a stronger group replaces it with another version of what works.

If Australian managers are determined to continue to promote humanistic values, it would seem that they condemn themselves to charges of mediocrity. Consequently, Australians are never sure whether they are managers or mates. And mates aren't sure how to respond to the increasing number of females in their midst. Is the age of managerial mateship coming to an inglorious end with the progressive feminising of management? Are the hard skills of management adequate to the task of managing in a postmodern world?

The term 'postmodernism' originated in 1960's literary criticism and is code for a farewell to reason. It is a sign of intellectual laziness and a symptom of a crisis of confidence in the Western rational tradition. Postmodernists laud the relativity of truth as a moral axiom and the failure of scientific rationality. In the 1970s the virus of postmodernism infected French and American academics and by the 1980s it had spread, plague-like, to Australian universities. There were dissenting voices who claimed that postmodernism was merely an undergraduate affectation which should not be able to fool rational thinkers. But since postmodernists reject rational thinking, argument and debate, the charge fell flat.

Postmodernists share a common project: to bury once and for all time the Enlightenment pursuit of truth, objectivity and reality. Their main target is objectivity, which is for them the grandest of all Western myths. The world simply does not exist as an independent entity but is an historically contingent product of local linguistic and community practices: the world is effectively created by language and society. There is no single world; there are as many worlds as there are languages and postmodernists. Happily asserting that truth is a word which forms part of a discredited language-game which once dominated Western thought, they conclude triumphantly that our experiences are not of facts but of 'narratives', or fairy-tales, with varying degrees of pragmatic value. In 2016, the Oxford dictionaries voted 'post-truth' as their word of the year!

Science, according to postmodernists, is no more objective than art and scientists engage in self-deceiving propaganda when they talk about value-neutrality in the pursuit of truth. Like American pragmatists, they eagerly embrace the view that all languages are equally valid, or invalid. Indeed, standards of validity do not apply: everything is relative, except the proposition 'everything is relative'.

Postmodernists assume that only absolute certainty allows us to talk of rational belief and since there is no absolute certainty, there are no good reasons to believe anything. They exhibit what Australian philosopher David Stove calls a 'disappointed perfectionism' which is associated with an irresponsible, frivolous levity. This form of (anti)thinking has led to widespread relativism and a general collapse of intellectual standards. How can one rationally respond to someone who believes that no principle of logic is rationally preferable to its denial?

Postmodernists delight in attacking and defaming authority figures, including managers and teachers, and thereby fail to distinguish between rational and irrational authority. Australian psychologists John Martin and John Ray showed that agreement with anti-rational authority statements was positively related to measures of emotional instability and negatively related to socio-economic status and intelligence.[10]

It is well known that authoritarianism is negatively related to intelligence, education and socio-economic class and positively related to ethnic prejudice and political conservatism. What is of prime importance is whether the authority to which one defers has or has not claims to rational support. Rejecting the right (rational) kind and accepting the (irrational) wrong kind of authority appear to be equally indicative of social and personal inadequacy. In this connection the relationships with intelligence are illuminating. Agreement with irrational authority and rejection of rational authority are both negatively related to intelligence, which means that people of low intelligence are likely to accept irrational authority and reject rational authority, so that they fail to discriminate between what is rational and what is not. In rejecting scientific rationality, postmodernists fail to distinguish between authoritarian and authoritative statements so that all authority figures are rejected, or at least regarded with the deepest suspicion. Historically, this attitude was laughed off as merely adolescent, as indeed it is.

To anyone with even a modicum of rationality, postmodern preciousness proves that something has gone seriously wrong with our thinking. Refusing to accept that there are facts, postmodernists will, like you and me, rush to a hospital with an inflamed appendix and willingly accept the truth of the diagnosis when life is threatened. They will not treat the doctor's factual language as merely expressive or part of a particular language-game and, like you and me, will participate in the very mature activity of asking questions, and perhaps even arguing with the doctor who wants to treat an inflamed appendix by removing their big toe.

By the 1990s postmodernism had infected the field of management. Modern organisations, which are mechanistic, objective and bureaucratic are to be replaced by postmodern organisations which are organic, subjective and democratic. Interpersonally, postmodernists prefer relationships to roles, networks to hierarchy, inspiration to orders, community to contracts, empathy to utility, happiness to performance, emotion to cognition and commitment to compliance. Educationally, postmodernists insist on teaching ignorance since they view education as indoctrination and want it to be empowering. Accordingly, professors and lecturers are replaced with postmodern 'facilitators' who are exceptionally modest in their disinclination to lecture, argue or reason. Theirs is a classroom in which feelings are shared in a spirit of empathy and relativistic modesty.

It would be unwise to claim that all managers who promote soft-skill management are postmodernists, even if it is true that they live in a postmodern world. In my experience, most managers are unfamiliar with the term and have little awareness of what postmodernists believe. Lucky managers! Yet, young managers, and especially females, are increasingly uncomfortable with the traditional approach to management. And human resource managers are in a position to do something about this state of affairs. Armed with degrees in psychology and postmodern consciousness, which embrace as many ideas as there are 'interesting' ones, they have changed the agenda of management training. Cognitive intelligence has given way to emotional intelligence and even spiritual intelligence. Personality has been brought into play to curb the excesses of the more boorish males. Autonomy has acquired a bad connotation while conviviality has been elevated to primary status. Political correctness is zealously enforced and those unfortunates who question the importance of 'sustainability', 'leadership', 'empowerment, 'stakeholders' or 'ethically sensitive management', are sentenced to the boondocks. Independence has been replaced by relationships and argument has given way to a cult of feeling.

In the last twenty years, the number of human resource managers increased markedly while the management education industry flourished as the number of MBA graduates increased. The management consulting industry grew dramatically and consultants began to play a significant role in restructuring businesses and promoting management discourse. By 1990, the Australian management consulting market was estimated to have an overall market value of $6.5 billion. Management was increasingly regarded as the professional success story of the late twentieth century and many young people sought entry to its corridors of wealth. Since managers need 'physicians of the soul' to help them manage effectively, human resource (HR) managers were given more power than they had enjoyed hitherto.

The Australian Human Resource Institute has over 20,000 members across Australia. Females represent sixty percent of total membership although that proportion can be expected to decrease as occupational health supervisors and 'team leaders' join the Institute. The rise to prominence of this once marginal activity began in the 1980s when personnel management, a predominantly male enclave for retired army officers and failed salesmen, was rebadged. HR academics claim that the difference between personnel management and HRM is reflected in the shift from: practice to values; monitoring to nurturing; negotiation to facilitation; and personnel procedures to cultural strategies. I will spare the reader the discouraging business of considering whether

HRM is 'strategic' in the way in which personnel management allegedly was not, which is news to those of us who worked in personnel departments in the 1970s.

As an aside, a management school once offered a four-week summer school in which every half-day was titled 'strategic': marketing, accounting, leadership, and so on. I was allocated a session at the end of the third week and, after introducing myself, announced that I taught 'strategic philosophy' and 'strategic psychology'. No one laughed.

The old personnel managers assumed that people have different values and goals and the manager's job is to resolve the inevitable conflicts. HR managers, it is said, assume that people can think and act collectively; their job is to coordinate people for common effort. In the former case, conflict is embraced and the prized managerial skill is negotiating. In the latter case, conflict is side-stepped and the managerial task is nurturing.

This new 'feminine' trend becomes even clearer with the debate between the practitioners of 'hard' and 'soft' HRM: the former associated with Taylorism and Peter Drucker and the latter with Elton Mayo and the human relations movement.

'Hard' HRM emphasises managerial prerogatives, the importance of bottom-line results and the preparedness of managers to take tough decisions. In contrast, 'soft' HRM emphasises the commitment, personality and motivation of employees. Each approach to management has developed its own language: 'hard' means objective, rational, analytic, tough-minded, impersonal, argumentative – masculine;

'soft' means subjective, intuitive, synthetic, tender-minded, personal, empathic – feminine.

Australians who enter the field of management face a dilemma, indeed a paradox. As they attempt to manage by performance, they find themselves confronted by a wall of resistance built upon local values. The danger is that the anti-authoritarian sentiment is exaggerated to include a generalised anti-authority attitude in which all authority figures are resisted. The paradox is that Australian managers need the authority to exercise power on behalf of their organisations, but are caught up in a postmodern society which has become more disdainful about authority generally. While it is rational to resist authoritarian managers, it is decidedly irrational to resist authoritative ones. The challenge for managers, therefore, is to convince others and themselves that they are indeed authoritative. And history shows us that, in Australia, this is not an easy challenge to meet.

Clearly, there is a tension in Australian management between 'hard' modern managers and 'soft' postmodern psycho-managers. The rise of psychomanagers has meant that hard-skill management is compromised by soft-skill management. Consequently, Australian managers are criticised for their insufficient commitment to work performance. It is of some interest, therefore, to discuss the work of the most influential advocate of management by performance and a trenchant critic of management by personality, Peter Drucker, and his debate with industrial psychologists.

3

THE GREAT DEBATE

Management: What managers do until they become leaders.

Leader: If a manager is someone with paid followers, then a leader is someone with unpaid followers who will jump over a cliff with them, or even for them.

Arguably, the great debate in twentieth-century management was between Peter Drucker and Abraham Maslow. Drucker believed that good management depends on whether the manager provides guidance in setting business goals and standards, while Maslow favoured the psychological health of the manager. Drucker believed that there is only one style of management: to make strength productive and weakness irrelevant. Maslow believed that a hierarchy of seven needs determines management style, although only five needs are taught to managers since the sixth and seventh are aesthetic and spiritual respectively. This may soon change given the intrusion into management training of spirit-seekers and other lost souls. Drucker believed that the key question in management is: 'What will they contribute?' Maslow thought it was: 'Will they get along with each other?' Drucker emphasised disagreement, argument and contribution; Maslow preferred agreement, harmony and motivation. Drucker believed that the role of psychology in management is to master oneself, not to control others; Maslow argued that psychology is the most important subject for managers to master and apply to others. Drucker emphasised the objective demands of the job; Maslow attended to the person's motivational state.

Drucker's popularity with Australian managers has, over five decades, run in inverse proportion to the popularity of management psychologists. While Drucker is rarely taught in detail, I am reliably informed that Australian MBA students are force-fed Maslow in the majority of their courses and Maslow's hierarchy of problems is better known than 'Waltzing Matilda'.

Born in 1909 in Vienna, Drucker studied economics and law before embarking on a career in journalism. From an early age he was determined to leave Austria and removed himself first to Germany where he met Doris, only to lose her, and then to England where he met her again. They married and settled in America in 1937 where Peter taught philosophy and politics at Bennington College in Vermont. From 1950 to 1972 he was Professor of Management at New York's Graduate School of Business and then Professor of Social Science at Claremont College in California. He died at his home in Claremont in November 2005.

In 1939 he published *The End of Economic Man* in which he tries to comprehend the appeal of fascism following the destruction of Europe's faith in an autonomous economic system, governed by rational laws and linked to liberty and equality. Fascism and Nazism succeeded because they were 'irrational' and based on a non-economic will to power. *The Future of Industrial Man* contains Drucker's vision of the central problems and challenges facing the industrial society which would follow the fall of totalitarianism, especially those of liberty and legitimacy. As Drucker saw the second half of the twentieth century, function and status would be determined by one's position in a large organisation in which a new and developing profession – management – would occupy a critical role. But he worried about the legitimacy of management and often upset business audiences by claiming that management is the second largest illegitimate profession and the first is fast becoming legitimate.

By the mid-1940s he was writing about management, but knew very little about what managers do. He needed to study managers but was unable to enter their domain. Then, in 1943, his luck changed and an invitation to study management practices at General Motors set him on the career for which he was to become famous. For two years he was able to talk with GM's senior managers, including the legendary Alfred Sloan. He had already formulated his view that managers have three jobs: to make economic resources productive (the entrepreneurial job); to make human beings productive (the administrative job); and to make public resources productive (the political job). He learned from GM's managers how they perform these jobs by setting objectives, integrating tasks and people, measuring performance and developing people by continuous learning. He admired the way GM's managers took responsibility for contribution and rewarded strong performance. He learned that managers are creators not controllers, and that 'leadership' is not about seducing people or appealing to one's personality. Rather, leadership is defined in terms of followers and it is the responsibility of managers to persuade others that they are worthy, on technical grounds, of being followed. It is simply irrational to follow people because of their personalities: that is the path to destruction.

Drucker learned from Sloan that the purpose of organisation is to make strength productive – and he never forgot it. He was never persuaded by the pleadings of human relations advocates who told him that what counts is job satisfaction. Indeed, he pointed to the evidence which showed conclusively that job satisfaction and job performance are not related. Many people who are dissatisfied with their jobs are strong performers whose dissatisfaction is 'creative energy'. He did not agree with those who believe that the major problem in management is ineffective communication. The three major dimensions of the task of management are: to think through and define the specific purpose of the organisation; to make work productive and employees achievers; and to manage social contacts and responsibilities. Since managers administer the present and create the future they have to be innovators rather than controllers.

Although Drucker was concerned about human satisfaction, he did not believe that it was necessary to have friendly relations with colleagues. Rather than emphasise 'management by getting on with others', he advocated management by objectives and self-control in order to produce responsibility and commitment within the organisation. Management by objectives and self-control encourages managers to develop a set of realistic objectives for their work group and for themselves. These objectives should spell out the contribution managers will make to the attainment of organisational goals in all areas of business. Management by objectives develops managerial self-control which, in turn, leads to stronger commitment and more efficient learning. Sadly, when MBO was applied to Australian organisations in the 1970s the moral emphasis on self-control was dropped and it became management by objectives and the manager's control.

Drucker learned from his study of GM that there are three forces of mismanagement: the specialised work of managers which encourages them to pursue specialised training rather than the general, humanistic education which is essential for community leadership; the existence of hierarchy, in which people define themselves as supervisors rather than managers; and confusion about the organisation's mission. Management by objectives and self-control can overcome these deficiencies by relating the task of each manager to the overarching goals of the business. Only by this technique can management become a cohesive group activity rather than a loose-knit collection of individuals pursuing their own agendas. Business failures are management and moral failures: they result from the lack of a cohesive management group and the lack of an overarching moral framework to regulate that group.

The business enterprise needs a principle of management that gives full scope to individual strength, a common direction to effort, and replaces external control with more effective internal control. However, Drucker believed that many managers have failed to take the initiative and in emphasising external control, they have failed to take advantage of the strengths of people. Employees in most companies are basically under-employed: their authority does not match their capacity. Employees must be held responsible for setting the goals for their own work and for managing themselves. This is not participative management, which is often only a futile attempt to disguise the reality of employee impotence through psychological manipulation. Imposing responsibility on employees – for continuous improvement in the performance of their own work – strengthens management because it creates a better understanding of management decisions and practices throughout the workforce.

Drucker also learned that, when taking important decisions, argument must be encouraged. In his wonderful autobiography, *Adventures of a Bystander*, Drucker tells his favourite story of Alfred Sloan endorsing an expensive and innovative proposal to his board only to have every board member politely agree with him. 'I take it all you gentlemen are in favour?' 'Yes, Mr. Sloan,' the chorus came back. 'Then I move that we defer action on this for a month to give ourselves a chance to think'.[1] A month later, after a robust debate, the proposal was rejected. Sloan and Drucker approved. Managers are not paid to share their feelings with each other: they are paid to give reasons to support their views. They are paid to argue and this crucial ability must be encouraged at all levels of the organisation.

In 1946 Drucker published an account of his study of GM. *Concept of the Corporation* became an immediate success and started the vogue for 'decentralisation'. Sloan immediately banned the book and forbade his executives to discuss it in his presence. Ford, on the other hand, embraced its ideas. When the young Henry Ford replaced his senile grandfather, he embraced *Concept of the Corporation* as his official text and gave Drucker the confidence to develop his ideas on management further. This he did in 1954 in his feisty book, *The Practice of Management*, which is widely regarded as his best management book and the first and last word on management.

Of all his work on management, Drucker considered his ideas about the self-governing plant community to be both the most important and the most original. Managers, however, have opposed these ideas as an 'encroachment' on their authority and trade unions have remained sceptical. Again, it was during his time at GM in the 1940s that he saw first-hand the possibilities for what became known as the Scandinavian semi- autonomous work group movement of the 1970s.

GM had successfully bid for a government contract which demanded highly skilled mechanics. Since there was no labour available in Detroit, two thousand black prostitutes were hired. On their arrival, they were shown a hastily-made training film and left to organise the work in their own way. Within a few weeks these unskilled, unsupervised illiterates were producing better work than skilled machinists had done before. Drucker argued that what was achieved in those factories in World War II went beyond the widely publicised Swedish experiments with semi- autonomous work groups in Volvo, Saab and elsewhere. And in these factories neither management nor trade unions suffered any impairment of authority or prosperity. Yet he was forced to concede that he was naive to expect that self-governing plant communities would be supported by managers and trade unionists. The movement towards autonomy at work failed: vested interests were, and remain, too powerful.

Drucker also participated in a workers' survey that was framed as a contest – "My Job and Why I Like It" – with many small prizes and judges to award them. The contest fully supported his assumptions, which were later popularised by Frederick Herzberg as the 'motivation-hygiene theory'. The results showed that the extrinsic rewards for work – pay or promotion – are what Herzberg called 'hygiene factors' because dissatisfaction with them is a powerful demotivator, but satisfaction with them is not especially important and an incentive to few. Achievement, contribution and responsibility are the powerful motivators. The survey also showed that employees want the chance to achieve at work and they particularly resent being prevented by meddlesome managers from doing the work for which they are paid.

Around 200,000 GM employees participated in the contest, but its success killed it. It was impossible to read, let alone collate, all the data and the union became so alarmed at the success of the contest that they made dropping further work on it a condition of accepting a wage settlement without a strike in 1948. And so the richest research material on employee attitudes and values ever collected was lost.

After the success of *The Practice of Management* in the mid- 1950s, Drucker became the most famous management consultant in America. Yet he was never tempted to become Peter Drucker Inc. He remained a 'one-man gunslinger' and surprised clients by delivering his 'reports' orally. As he was leaving, a client asked whether he would submit a written report. Drucker was clearly amused and offered to throw in sex and violence to make this unnecessary task more interesting. He was often accused of making 'facts' up and basing his recommendations on anecdotes and novels. His widow, Doris, told me that he wanted to be a gentleman in the style of a Jane Austen character and one can see him in his later years as a playful Mr Bennett. A master of the witty aphorism and a masterful storyteller, he nonetheless was wary of the management fads and fashions that followed him. He never accepted the emphasis that managers place on 'potential' since we have all been on promises. He emphasised performance over potential and was especially opposed to assessing potential by psychometric tests. He was equally sceptical about managers' obsession with leadership: 'leadership' often means the ability to bewitch the led.

According to Drucker, business has only two functions: marketing and innovation. Sadly, managers are obsessed with organisational restructures ('organitis'). After several decades in the consulting business, he concluded that far too much reorganisation goes on. He compared organitis to a spastic colon and organisational restructures to surgery: one doesn't just cut. He may have been one of management's greatest supporters but he was always ready to offer constructive criticism. It may surprise many people to hear him say that so much of what we call management consists in making it difficult for people to work. He noted wistfully that job enrichment has been around for more than sixty years and while it has been successful every time it has been tried, managers are not interested. As for management by objectives: it works if managers know the objectives but ninety percent of the time they don't.

He retained a constructive scepticism about professions. He advised his clients not to put the fate of their business in the delusions of economists. He reminded them that there are no good executive compensation plans: there are only bad and worse ones. Many of his clients thought he was frivolous when he told them that if they wanted to hire fifty people under the age of 25, they should hire double that number at random and six months later sell the worst fifty to their competitors. If they wanted to hire people over the age of 25, the only criterion for selection should be the person's successful performance in the last job(s).

Drucker was, however, a defender of the most maligned man in management classrooms. If managers and their teachers do not like a writer it is usually because he is a critic of their profession. Most of the management icons are sympathetic to the plight of managers and believe that they generally act rationally and wisely. Any writer who believes that managers are generally irrational, status-seeking, power-hungry individuals who make it difficult for people to do their work is a strong candidate for infamy. There was such a man – Frederick Taylor – and to the surprise of many of his students and clients, Drucker defended him.

In the nineteenth century managers were largely concerned with production techniques and the problems of financial control. The human aspects of work were either ignored or given little credence. Among the developments that forced managers to think in wider terms was bureaucratisation. As the size of business organisations grew, managers began to think of problems of employee morale and communication, lines of authority and the control of large numbers of people. Managers also had to cope with the loss of individual power: no longer did one individual control the organisation. Individual desires were tempered by committees and conferences, which led to a desire to understand the psychological aspects of workplace behaviour.

Frederick Winslow Taylor, the founding father of the 'science of work', loathed inefficiency and management incompetence. In 1912 he described US Steel's managers as shameful and deplorable. He believed managers were generally incompetent because they lacked information about their employees' abilities and the time required to perform their work. He saw that managers arbitrarily designed jobs which encouraged employees to collude to achieve reduced time rates. Managers were selfish, ignorant and irrational. Workers, on the other hand, generally pursued rational strategies of self-interest. Given a hostile and difficult work environment, Taylor found it easy to understand go-slow tactics and self-interested behaviour. He believed that many of these problems could be solved by the application of scientific principles to workplace behaviour, since science enables engineers to capitalise on employees' rationality by establishing objective standards for such behaviour. The first step was to study work time, individual work movements, fatigue factors, job routines, work sequences and the timing of rest pauses. Work analysis was, therefore, to form part of an overall scheme which would replace arbitrary work design with scientific principles. Taylor died during the early phase of this ambitious program.

Taylor's writings on 'scientific management', including his five-day Testimony in 1912 before a Committee of the House of Representatives, are reprinted in *Scientific Management*. His Testimony presented his mature views and demonstrated his obsession with substituting industrial harmony for industrial warfare. This would require increasing wages, decreasing physical stress, developing the human being and replacing 'bosses' with 'servants of workmen' whose duty is to help workers perform more effectively.

Programs for increasing the productivity of labour through techniques of time, motion and cost analysis were reinforced by the assumption that the major motivating force for employees (and managers) is money, and this resulted in an emphasis on wages, incentives and a 'fair day's work for a fair day's pay'. Taylor and his disciples viewed payment by results programs and incentive bonuses as adequate compensation for whatever constraints on human satisfaction such techniques might generate. The bad news for managers was that they were supposed to allow some workers to earn more money than they were receiving, since Taylor insisted that there should be no limit to the earnings of high-output workers. This they were not prepared to do. To be fair to Taylor, it should be remembered that he warned managers that financial rewards were only a partial answer to the problem of employee motivation.

It is standard practice for management writers to criticise Taylor. Indeed, he has few defenders. One notable exception was Drucker who argued that there are few cases in intellectual history where what a person actually said and did, and what he is generally believed to have said and done, are so totally at variance.[2] Taylor was not solely interested in profits and costs and he did not invent and subordinate workers to the production line. And he definitely did not want to put more power into the hands of managers. Rather, his central concern was to achieve industrial harmony through higher productivity. He believed that workers should receive the full benefit of higher productivity, whether in the form of higher wages or shorter hours of work – and that financial incentives were necessary but not sufficient to motivate workers. He wanted to replace the 'boss' with what is known as matrix organisation. Contrary to popular belief, hierarchical organisation structures run counter to Taylor's principles. He never hesitated to criticise managers who wanted to centralise power in their own hands. Why, then, has Taylor been so totally misrepresented?

Drucker dismissed the facile suggestion that Taylor was a 'captive of nineteenth-century psychology' which was influenced by social Darwinism and a general belief that social reforms should be grounded on maximising industrial output through hard work and the application of scientific principles. On the contrary, Taylor was ahead of his time in anticipating the psychological theories of McGregor and Herzberg. Yet he was rejected and ridiculed by university professors and by the ideologues of the Left and Right. He died before he could turn his attention to senior managers and we can only ponder what he would have made of today's managers. Have they learned from Taylor about the complicated relationship between money, motivation and manipulation?

A case in point was Henry Ford who, in 1914, doubled the wages of his employees in an attempt to 'hold the workers'. Ford found, however, that staff turnover had risen again by 1918. The cost of living had risen by seventy-eight per cent above the 1914 level, although Ford had not increased wages. Instead, he lectured his employees about loyalty and gratitude. Finally, in 1920, the Ford profit-sharing plan was abandoned and the search was on for a different approach to employee motivation. The Hawthorne studies were to provide the new emphasis. And it was the Hawthorne researchers who radically modified management ideology. Henceforth, Taylor would be portrayed as the 'bad boy' of industrial work and a new band of social scientists insinuated themselves into management. They became known as the 'human relations school' and their influence was, and continues to be, staggering.

The father of the human relations movement was an Australian, Elton Mayo, who popularised the Hawthorne studies. These infamous studies were conducted between the mid-1920s and the late-1930s at the Hawthorne plant of the Western Electric Company in Chicago. The researchers attached limited importance to formal organisation and technology and emphasised the informal relationships between people at work, especially conditions for sociability and belongingness. The emphasis was linked to Mayo's view that the basic problem of industrial society is best defined as the severance of the social links that characterise preindustrial society. As increased anomie at work was seen as the problem, researchers attempted to generate a social environment around the individual.

The key findings which emerged from the Hawthorne studies provided major themes for human relations writers in their search for supportive work environments: the importance of social norms; the significance of non-economic rewards; the influence of informal groups; the role of leadership in enforcing group norms; and the importance of participation in decision making. The Hawthorne researchers concluded that there was no evidence that workers are primarily motivated by economic interests, and the efficacy of a wage incentive was so dependent on its relation to other factors that it was impossible to consider it as having an independent effect on workers.

Sydney psychologist Alex Carey concluded that there is no evidence for such conclusions.[3] He also criticised the Hawthorne researchers for their refusal to consider the power relationships that defined the work environment. To recognise the power relationships in the factory is to acknowledge the existence of conflicting interests, which the researchers failed to admit or consider. The researchers also ignored the existence of trade unions throughout the study, because they were unnecessary. This capacity to ignore management-union relationships is amazing when it is remembered that from 1933–1936, according to a 1937 U.S. Senate Committee, Western Electric's managers paid $26,000 to spies commissioned to report on and subvert union involvement among employees. It is clear that an anti-union, pro-management bias permeated all those who were involved in the nine-year research program so that interpretations of their findings should be treated with care, to say the least, in the most charitable fashion. The other important consequence of the neglect of power relationships, aided by the severity of the economic depression, concerned the status of money as a motivating factor. A demand by workers for higher wages would constitute a conflict of interest and so power relationships would have to be considered. As this was to be avoided within the research, emphasis was displaced from economic incentives to social relationships.

Why such claims as those of the Hawthorne researchers should have gained widespread acceptance is a question in need of an answer. Carey concluded that there are no grounds in the objective content of the records of the Hawthorne studies for their authors' conclusions. The data from these studies, far from supporting the human relations approach, are surprisingly consistent with a rather old-world view about the value of monetary incentives, driving management and discipline.

Alex Carey was a major figure on the Sydney industrial psychology scene, especially in the 1960s and 70s. His radical critiques of mainstream industrial psychology unsettled and upset managers and ensured that his status would be that of an eccentric outsider. He was a liberal humanist and an inspiring educator but had little time for students who wanted merely to be trained. He arrived for our first class with hair dripping from saltwater and told his blue-suited managers that we could leave immediately if we thought he was going to tell us how to make money by manipulating others. He was one of the best teachers I ever had, and after I graduated from the University of NSW, we became casual friends.

In 1987 we were to share a lecture platform at the then Kuringai College of Advanced Education. My reluctance to participate in the seminar vanished when I heard that Alex would be attending. He was known for his casual attitude toward appointments and so we were not surprised when he failed to show up by the session's appointed start time. We were to learn later that at the very time he was scheduled to speak to the audience, he hanged himself.

In the field of management Alex Carey is especially remembered for his critiques of the Hawthorne studies. He is also known for his critique of the classic study of autocratic and democratic supervisory styles conducted by Kurt Lewin, a refugee from Nazi Germany who went to America determined to promote the ideals of democracy in all its forms. He drew a sharp distinction between democratic and autocratic styles of supervision and sought evidence for the superiority of the former.[4] He argued that autocrats: determine policies themselves and dictate techniques and activities intermittently so that future steps are always uncertain; are personal in their praise and criticism of the work of group members; remain aloof from active group participation except when demonstrating tasks. Democrats: encourage group discussion and decision; sketch general steps to achieve group goals; suggest possible courses of actions; allow people to work with whomever they choose; are objective in their praise and criticism; try to be a regular member of the group in spirit without taking over the work of others.

It is widely believed that Lewin's studies found that the democrats developed higher levels of 'morale' in their groups than did the autocrats. Further, it is generally accepted that the democratically-managed groups achieved the higher level of output. There have been few major criticisms of this study and again it was Alex Carey who showed that the results point to the conclusion that the autocratic groups produced less aggression and higher levels of output than did the democratic groups.[5]

The Lewinian researchers made it a condition of autocracy that the supervisor only revealed to group members the steps to the group goal one at a time, whereas in the democratic condition the path to the group goal was a matter of discussion and decision. But the lack of a group goal is not fundamental to autocracy. Totalitarian governments often make the goals of their countries quite explicit while in some democracies social goals are frequently unclear. One thinks of Hitler's openness about his plans for domination and John F. Kennedy's secrecy about Cuba.

Australian psychologists Adrienne Hall and Pat Bazely repeated the Lewinian studies, paying particular attention to goal clarity. Hall, for example, examined the relationship between group morale, effectiveness and supervisory style when goal perspective was equally clear in both autocratic and democratic conditions. She found that there was no difference in morale between the groups. Autocratic groups, however, produced higher levels of output. These results, in conjunction with those of Bazely, offer convincing evidence that clarity of goal perspective rather than supervisory style was the major variable in Lewin's study.[6]

Carey and Drucker were particularly sceptical of the 'human relations' and democratic supervision movements. Drucker claimed that the human relations movement grew out of attempts to subvert the growth of trade unions by pretending that managers cared about the psychological needs of their employees. In a 1950 article, he argued that:

> The human relations policies which American management had been buying wholesale in the past ten years have been a conspicuous waste and failure in my opinion...Most of us in management . . . have instituted them as a means of busting the unions. That has been the main theme of these programs. They are based on the belief that if you have good employee relations the union will wither on the vine.[7]

The intrusion into management of this form of psychology was dangerous and had the potential to undermine managerial power. While Drucker acknowledged that people had different personalities and needs, he was not convinced that personality or motivational factors should determine how managers relate to their colleagues. And he vigorously opposed the use of psychological interviews and psychometric tests. This did not mean that he ignored good manners. Working with people is difficult, but not impossible. Tax accountants aren't going to change, but at least they can learn to say 'good morning'. He believed that if managers spend more than ten percent of their time on 'human relations' they have time on their hands. And to depend on human resource managers to do management development is a misunderstanding: it is the job of managers to develop their staff.

It was during the 1950s that some psychologists worried about the management bias of their colleagues and reversed the traditional position. Instead of trying to show managers how to induce workers to work harder and more harmoniously for less money, they insisted that money was the single greatest incentive. The cycle had been completed. This time managers, following Ford's lead, were not quite as receptive to the 'money' argument. Rather, new approaches were eagerly sought. Personality and intelligence testing, variations on the Hawthorne studies, sensitivity groups, communication techniques, worker participation schemes and a host of managerial fads invaded workplaces. Little attention was given to such subjects as merit-rating schemes, incentive payment systems or wage review programs. The human relations movement may have passed into the human resources movement but its legacy remained. Never again would managers emphasise the motivating power of money. They had flirted with psychologists and they were now ready seriously to embrace them. Psychologists returned the favour and set their sights on the old guard, notably Taylor and Drucker.

Drucker was criticised by psychologists, including Maslow and McGregor, for failing to appreciate and account for individual differences, especially personal needs. Drucker addressed this issue in his 1977 best-seller, *Management*, by criticising industrial psychologists for their simplistic accounts of workplace behaviour and their habit of pretending that descriptions of everyday behaviour are universal theories of human nature.

Douglas McGregor had argued that when managers take decisions they make assumptions about human behaviour which reflect their commitment to one of two schools of thought: scientific management or human relations. Theory X represents the traditional, scientific management approach which assumes that most people have an inherent dislike of work which they will strive to avoid at all cost. They work to satisfy physiological and safety needs, primarily through financial gain and since they are motivated by the threat of punishment, they must be coerced and controlled in order to ensure effective performance. Theory X takes no heed of individuals' personal desires to achieve self-respect or self-actualisation. Theory Y, which is more akin to the human relations school, assumes that people will exercise self-control in working towards objectives to which they are committed. It assumes that most people strive for personal growth and responsibility and are motivated by esteem and self-actualisation needs which, if met, satisfy both personal and organisational ends. In short, Theory X assumes immaturity and Theory Y assumes that people want to be adults. Although McGregor presented these theories as viable alternatives, it is clear that he committed himself to Theory Y.

Drucker acknowledged that McGregor's 1960 book *The Human Side of Enterprise* was (for the next two decades) the most widely-read and most often quoted book in the field of industrial psychology. McGregor's research revealed that organisations which were low in efficiency tended to be controlled by people who were 'job centred'. They concentrated on keeping their subordinates busily engaged in a specified work cycle, at a satisfactory rate, determined by time standards. By contrast, the best performances were found in organisations where supervisors focused on the human aspects of their subordinates' problems and saw their role as helping them to do their work effectively. The supervisors who employed a Theory Y approach exercised a general rather than a detailed control over the job and were more concerned with targets than methods. They had high performance goals but allowed maximum participation in decision making and were 'employee' rather than 'job' centred.

Drucker used one psychologist to criticise another. He pointed out that Maslow had spent a year working with a small company in California which tried to practice Theory Y and discovered that the demand for responsibility and achievement sometimes exceeded what any but the strong and healthy person could take. He criticised Theory Y for 'inhumanity' toward weak and vulnerable people who cannot take on the self-discipline which Theory Y demands. He rejected McGregor's assumption that most people want to be adults: he thought many want to remain immature. Maslow concluded, and Drucker agreed, that while Theory Y is superior to Theory X, managers have to replace the security of the latter with a different structure of security which goes well beyond it. Theory Y cannot simply be substituted for Theory X: it has to go far beyond it. He concluded that the debate over the validity of Theory X versus Theory Y is a sham battle. The question managers need to ask is not, 'which theory of human nature is the correct one?' Rather, the right question is: 'what is the reality of my situation and how can I discharge my task of managing subordinates?'

Throughout his professional life Drucker defended the practice of management against the 'psychological despots'. Using psychology to control and manipulate others is, for him, a self-destructive abuse of knowledge and a particularly repugnant form of tyranny: the master of old was content to control the slave's body.

For example, managers who pretend that colleagues' need for affection - rather than the objective needs of the task- determine what should be done are poor managers. All they do is to destroy the integrity of the relationship and with it the respect for their person and function. And those managers who claim the status of leadership should be regarded with the deepest suspicion.

Drucker was ambivalent, if not sceptical, about man- agers' obsession with 'leadership'. In his best-selling book *Management*, 'leadership' does not appear in the Index. There are effective and ineffective managers and apparent- ly there are also leaders. But what is the difference between an effective manager and a managerial leader? Is the current rage for leadership another example of management-babble? Why do we need to add another, tendentious concept to a field over-burdened with jargon?

In a 1988 article Drucker acknowledges that 'leadership is all the rage just now' and is amused when a HR manager asks him to run a seminar on how one acquires charisma. He tells the naïve manager that leaders think through their organisation's mission, define and establish it, set goals, priorities and maintain standards. Leaders see leadership as responsibility rather than as rank and privilege. Leaders strive to earn trust because without which there will be no followers. When he finished this summary, the HR manager said: 'But that's no different from what we have known for years are the requirements for being an effective manager'. Precisely.[8]

Rulers throughout history have wanted to believe that others obeyed them, not because they had the power to enforce obedience, but because they were 'born leaders'. This myth was invented by Plato and has been so successful that it is still debated seriously in business schools. In *The Republic*, Plato called the story of the 'born leader' the great lordly lie and advised rulers to use it to legitimise their power. He argued that with the help of one audacious lie, rulers may, if they are lucky, persuade even themselves. It seems that politicians, bureaucrats and managers have been persuaded that leaders are born and not made since for decades they have been obsessed with leadership. Their fascination with leadership is based on a desire, rarely stated openly, to believe that their power derives from colleagues' recognition of their exemplary personalities.

The way in which the notion of leadership has been used by psychologists and management consultants in industry and government has been well documented by Loren Baritz in *The Servants of Power*. He argued that the early formulations insisted that leadership was an art, something vague and even mystical that could not be reduced to scientific investigation or communicated to managers. According to this view, leaders are born and not made, a view which is closely related to the popular idea that leadership is a function of personality. Leaders were thought to have strong characters, self-confidence, sensitivity, integrity and imagination. This contradicted research which showed that about fifty percent of successful executives have volatile tempers and do not know, like or care about their colleagues. It was not until after the Second World War that managers embraced the view that authoritarian leadership in management was likely to fail, since the consent of the managed was essential to success. Subordinates needed to be persuaded rather than ordered to behave appropriately. Power was not to be used where persuasion might work. And persuasion meant the ability to convince workers of the wisdom of management decisions. According to Baritz, this concern with leadership became a fetish after the 1950s. Conferences were dominated by the topic and speeches regularly emphasised the need to transform management into leadership. Managers like to think that subordinates obey them because they are 'gifted visionaries', not because they have the power to enforce obedience. In short, out of the desire of managers to be respected as persons, rather than as powers, grew an industry which continues to go from strength to strength. Leadership remains one of the most popular topics on the management training circuit and psychologists continue to write books about the personalities of leaders.

It is obvious that the leaders of the twentieth century had different personalities and were, alas, human-all-too-human. Indeed, their emotional instability and deficiencies as human beings encourage us to wonder how they became leaders. Management writers on leadership avoid unsavoury characters and offer sanitised descriptions of the lives of their heroes. Many, however, continue to subject readers to lists of leadership 'traits' in spite of the fact that psychologists have singularly failed to produce any meaningful results. The personality trait approach to the study of leadership – based on inferences from leader behaviour – faces the challenge of explaining the behaviour of followers, and it runs into insuperable problems. The search for stable and enduring personal qualities of leaders has failed, and must fail, because leaders cannot be understood apart from their relationship with their followers. Both must be considered partners in the game of leadership and it is invalid to analyse one party at the expense of the other: leaders cannot exist without followers.

Managers are no longer uncontested figures. In recent years they are, as we say in Australia, decidedly 'on the nose'. Journalists call them 'bosses' and many people sneeringly refer to them as 'suits'. They are increasingly criticised for their refusal to acknowledge the moral nature of their activities and so the question of morality of ends, and therefore of management effectiveness in achieving those ends, is rarely discussed. We should not be surprised, therefore, that they try to legitimise themselves by appealing to their 'leadership qualities' or exemplary personalities. However, they are not able to explain the difference between an effective manager and a leader.

Wittgenstein argued that the meaning of a word depends on its role in the language game of which it is a member.

The words 'manager' and 'leader' operate in quite different language games, as managers know only too well. That they (and others) want us to believe they are leaders by invoking a language game which includes the ideas of gifted and superior individuals leading others on a journey to paradise, would appeal to Plato and to Machiavelli. But history tells us that leaders are just as (if not more) likely to lead us to hell.

Drucker set himself against those psychologists who treat people as bundles of relatively-fixed dispositions – personality traits and psychological needs. He was a sort of existentialist who believed that humans are strategic beings who strive for autonomy but must also be part of society. He was fond of the father of Christian existentialism, Danish philosopher Soren Kierkegaard, who believed that human existence is possible only in perpetual tension between the individual's autonomous existence and as a citizen in society.[9] Like Kierkegaard, Drucker reasserted the existence of individuals against the social conditions which threaten to encapsulate them and he rejected the notion of personality as a psychological trap which submerges individuals in biological and social structures. Humans are never devoid of choice and are therefore responsible for the consequences of their choices, insofar as they are aware of them.

Management is neither science nor art. It is a practice and it can be taught. But training is not enough. Managers need to be educated for positions of community responsibility and for more than two thousand years it has fallen to the liberal arts to achieve this noble goal. So when Drucker retired from New York University he chose to continue to teach at a liberal arts college in California. To retire was, for him, a death sentence; and since he loved to teach, he continued into his nineties to face classes of respectful students. He remained to the end of his life a teacher of rare wit, intelligence and insight into the discipline of management, a discipline which he largely created. He believed that his greatest strength as a consultant was to ask a few basic questions. If a client leaves a room feeling he has learned a lot, Drucker concluded that the client is either stupid or he had done a bad job.

4

MOTIVATION AND MANIPULATION

Moving Forward: a phrase used by managers to keep one word ahead of their colleagues who are merely moving.

Manipulation: Comes between managing director and manual worker.

Motive is a term which has had a variety of meanings in the course of history. In *Othello*, Shakespeare thought of 'motive' as a force: 'a moving or exciting cause', rather than a reason for action. In ordinary discourse the word 'motive' covers both meanings: force and reason. Enquiries about motive ordinarily mean that we are dealing with a human being rather than a mechanical object. We do not ask what the motive of a car might be. Furthermore, an enquiry about motive assumes that choice is within the capacity of individuals. If we ask about a person's motive for living, we assume that he is continuing at his own choice.

Shakespeare's idiosyncratic use of motive as force has become the rule in psychology, where it is assumed that all behaviour is caused by forces. Consequently, most concepts in psychology have acquired a pushing or pulling component.

Hence the topic of 'motivation', which deals in forces under a variety of names – motives, traits, instincts, drives and needs. While there is an implicit analogy with the concept of force in Newtonian physics, there is also an echo of the metaphorical uses to which we put the term 'force' in everyday life: 'I am forced to earn my living', for example. This metaphorical usage merely implies that one's choice is restricted by circumstances. However, the use of the term in psychology implies that, say, deprivation of status causes individuals to seek status in the same way as the force of gravity causes a pen to fall if dropped.

An important point about motive-forces in psychology is that they are irredeemably circular. We observe a woman crying and infer a motive-force which is compelling her to do just that. But this is a tautological explanation, not an empirical truth. Of course, it has the added advantage that she cannot be held responsible for her (strategic) behaviour. (It has to be admitted that nowadays popular explanations would refer the causes of her crying to hormones or brain chemicals, but that is another story).

Some psychologists have pointed out that the problem of motivation is a pseudo-problem – since explanation of the fact that human beings are active is not necessary. It can be taken that they are active and the problem is one of explaining the direction taken by action. When I worked in a psychology department many years ago, there was a proposal put to the faculty to introduce a course on 'motivation'. After acrimonious debate, the proposal was rejected on the grounds that there was nothing to teach since motives are not forces inside people, but reasons for human actions which are embedded in their social context. For example, there is an important difference between blinking and winking. While blinking is reactive, individuals have reasons for winking, or given the current politically-correct environment, not winking.

Like psychologists, managers have eagerly embraced the idea that motives are forces which propel people into action, because it appears to provide them with scientific means by which their colleagues may be understood and controlled. If scientists control nature, why can't psychologists and managers control human behaviour?

Abraham Maslow's influential motivational theory shows clearly how the idea of 'motive as cause' has been useful in allowing people to deny their personal responsibilities. Maslow's popularity with Australian managers is based on his theory of personality which depends on the notion of a hierarchy of needs. In *Motivation and Personality* he insists that people are moved by needs on several levels, which are defined such that no need belonging to a higher level comes into operation until the needs of all inferior levels have been satisfied. At the top of Maslow's hierarchy are notions like self-esteem and self-actualisation, which cannot be seen as motive-forces without doing considerable violence to the word 'need'. Everyday talk would regard self-esteem as a desirable state to achieve, whereas Maslow claimed that we are driven towards it after certain subordinate goals have been achieved.

Maslow's motivational theory combined deprivation-and growth-motivation into his hierarchy of needs (independent of ends). This contrasted with the prevailing view, which regarded motivation as a series of separate drives. Maslow identified seven basic needs (although only five are commonly taught to managers) in ascending order of importance: physiological needs (hunger, thirst, fatigue); security needs (protection against danger); social needs (friendship, affection, intimacy); esteem needs (status, reputation, mastery); self-actualisation needs (achievement, creativity); aesthetic needs (beauty, art) and metaphysical needs (Platonic ideas). A motive at a lower level is more powerful than one at a higher level. As teachers of Maslow's motivational theory rarely discuss the sixth and seventh levels, attention is directed to his five-tier model and his conceptual sleight of hand.

Maslow imputed to all individuals the push toward actualisation of inherent potentialities. But he also recognised another tendency: a push to satisfy needs ensuring physical and psychological survival. The former push is toward fulfilment; the latter primary push is toward assistance. According to Maslow, the survival and actualisation tendencies are necessary for a mature, meaningful life. Incomplete or faulty self-actualisation can lead to psychological problems, including mental illness, which Maslow thought of as a 'deficiency disease': an inability of individuals to satisfy their unfulfilled needs.

Maslow's psychology is hedonistic: individuals make choices on the basis of what is satisfying to their bodies and sense of wellbeing. Individuals do not self-consciously choose to actualise their potentialities; their decisions are based on what is satisfying, what they need. Individuals need self-actualisation and they choose self-actualisation because they need to. This proposition is invalid because it is circular. And Maslow's emphasis on the importance to all individuals of a hierarchy of needs, which governs physiological and psychological aspects of their existence, does not solve this problem. Rather, it begs the question: what is a 'need'?

It is obvious that physiological needs represent the primary drives being concerned with hunger, thirst, sleep, relaxation and bodily integrity. Safety needs call for a predictable and orderly world: safe, reliable and consistent. While these are not satisfied people will be occupied in attempts to organise their world to provide the greatest possible security and safety, which imply interactions with other people. If satisfied, they come under the force of social needs, which emphasise love and belongingness and so depend entirely on levels of social interaction. Esteem needs imply that one's subjective assessment of achievement is important because these needs are concerned with the desire for strength, achievement, adequacy, mastery, competency, confidence, independence, reputation and prestige.

Self-actualisation shifts the meaning of need because its aim is unspecifiable. These needs include the full use and exploitation of talents, capacities and potentialities. Self-actualisers are able to submit to social regulation without losing their integrity or personal independence, although they are constantly evaluating other possibilities. They aim to develop to the full stature of which they are capable.

Maslow's claim that if one has satisfied lower needs (and not otherwise) one will necessarily proceed to the higher steps of the motivational ladder has important implications for personal development. By deduction, those who have had their physiological and safety needs satisfied throughout their life will inevitably become those who develop their higher potentialities. So those raised in relative luxury will become more creative and integrated personalities; those raised in disadvantageous circumstances will end up as inferior products. Facts do not bear this out. It is patently untrue that one must attend to the lower levels before the higher. Martyrs have pursued self-actualisation under the certainty of death.

Furthermore, Maslow's use of 'need' changes as one proceeds up the hierarchy. What begins as a physiological necessity becomes a psychological need (which does not imply necessity). Food is necessary to survival; self-actualisation is not. At the lower levels the aim of the need is specifiable (e.g. survival); at the highest levels it is not. The notion of self-actualisation points toward the integrated individual but there is no criterion for recognising one of these. Since this motive cannot be inferred from behaviour which leads to a recognisable goal, Maslow regarded it as a 'push' motive arising within the person. Push motivation originates in the tendency of a person's physiology to function according to its design and to develop to the fullest. Failure to exercise one's powers results in irritation; success is followed by pleasure. Maslow suggested that humans are 'set' to self-actualise by virtue of their physiological make-up just as a sunflower seed is 'set' by its make-up to grow into a plant. Social conditions can influence the result but people are basically persistent developers of their potential.

It is obvious that Maslow could not logically hold this position. One cannot operate logically within a hierarchy in which some motives are goal-orientated and based on deprivation (like sex), while others are not. Furthermore, the admission of a self-actualising tendency in humans cannot fairly be placed on the same level as sunflowers, which do not have intentions or make choices for which they are responsible. Since one cannot eradicate the consciousness of purpose, choice and responsibility from humans (excepting some psychologists), Maslow's attitude to these concepts is unconvincing. The notion of actualisation of potentialities devoid of purpose is appropriate for thinking about sunflowers, but self-actualisation can only apply to humans and one cannot claim that it is without purpose.

The popularity of Maslow's hierarchy of needs seems to be based on the recognition that we do indeed organise ourselves to satisfy basic needs before attending to sophisticated pursuits and that it is rational to do so unless circumstances dictate otherwise. It may be the case that many people who respond positively to Maslow's theory do not interpret 'need' to mean motive-force, preferring the everyday notion of 'reason'. A lay view would be that Maslow was talking about ways of emancipating ourselves from necessity. Consequently, one might advance Maslow's hierarchy as a statement about what a rational society should aim to provide for its members. Or one might see it as a value hierarchy that individuals could choose to follow in organising their own activities. The response to Maslow's hierarchy is frequently one of familiarity, which stems from the way it echoes the everyday notion that one category of needs is more vital than another.

Where motivational theories employ the notion of motive-force as the basis for a mechanistic model, problems of circularity, inconsistency, intentionality, freedom of choice and responsibility make it unlikely that they can explain anything at all. The case against Maslow is not so clear-cut because he uses the safety valve of self-actualisation to open a window to freedom and responsibility. It is for this reason that he was widely regarded as a member of a 'third force' of psychologists who disagreed with the strict determinism of psychoanalysis and behaviourism. When confronted by motivational psychologists it is important, therefore, to be clear about their use of 'motive'.

In Maslow's case, it is possible to remove the notion of motive and admit that individuals make choices on rational grounds. This culminates in the recognition of the 'motive hierarchy' itself as a rough set of priorities for action, both personal and social, such as would be arrived at on rational grounds. A rational society would aim to emancipate its people from needs, in something like the order of priority set by Maslow's hierarchy, or by Epicurus (341–270 BC). First, it would attend to the matter of securing its members against the necessities for food, shelter and the depredations of competitors, and then it would attend to sheltering the process of procreation and child-rearing; with this base secured it would provide for the more civilised amenities of creativity, artistry, science. This is an outline reminiscent of Utopia. It appears inescapable that Maslow's theory of human nature is based on his observation of forms of social organisation and their rational manipulation.

It is one thing to say that people have reasons to pursue particular goals and quite another to say that people are made to pursue those goals by some mysterious inner force. Motive-as-reason implies choice and responsibility; motive-as-cause does not. Motive-as-reason refers to that which justifies the choice of an intention to act so that it narrows the possible choices open to one. One may also form the intention of acting without there being any motive (reason) to warrant the choice. Choice is free.

The tendency to mishandle the concept of motive is especially prominent among psychiatrists who, like lawyers, are almost always compelled to deal with motives in hindsight. For example, a vandal may be told by a psychiatrist that his 'real motive' for destroying public property is to injure his father. The vandal has probably never entertained such an idea, although he can quickly appreciate its favourable consequences for him. And so he readily accepts this 'explanation'. The psychiatrist's improper position is revealed if he meets someone whose reply is: 'Yes, I realised that my father might suffer, but my motive was so strong that I had no choice but to take the chance because I want to be accepted by my friends.'

The psychiatrist's method may be successful up to a point. Revealing to the vandal the consequences of his actions, convincing him that others will hold him responsible for effects he did not intend and helping him see the wisdom of thinking before acting may be effective educational acts, regardless of the psychiatric tricks used. But the cost is high because they enmesh him in a morass of linguistic obfuscation. Surely it would be better to educate vandals about how actions have unintended consequences and how responsibility is attributed.

Maslow's hierarchy is not a true model of human behaviour since there are many instances in which individuals appear to be motivated by needs at the higher levels when the needs they should have at the lower level are not satisfied. A fugitive who is hungry is not forced to eat before attempting to evade his captors. As a theory of a hierarchy of motive-forces, Maslow's has to be rejected. He appears to have recognised this and acknowledged that in practice most people experience a mixture of satisfactions at any one time, so the separate levels of needs cannot be taken literally. The main point that emerges from Maslow's theory, however, is that higher order needs are not usually significant until basic needs have been met.

Why, then, is Maslow's theory so popular with Australian managers? I suggest that in management circles this view of human behaviour has been used as a powerful justification for emphasising social relationships and communication skills rather than attending to employees' demands for more control over their jobs. If social needs are not satisfied – and we might ask whether they can be satisfied in work relationships – there is no point in encouraging employees to pursue personal power, let alone self-actualisation. Similarly, management problems can be defined in terms of 'poor communication' –

which they frequently are – while ignoring the substantive content of the communications.

Most management textbooks written after 1950 emphasise the importance of social needs and it is hard to quarrel with writers who profess care and concern for the social well-being of working people. Indeed, it is unwise in management circles to suggest that a sleight of hand may be at work and that Maslow's theory has been used brilliantly as a servant of power by allowing managers to direct resources to training in interpersonal skills and personality assessment, rather than job enrichment.

The important issue, however, is not whether Maslow's theory is popular but whether it is adequate. The best support for Maslow's theory comes from studies which suggest that if we decrease hierarchical control we will obtain what Maslow calls self-actualising behaviour. This should not surprise us since Maslow's theory was derived from observations of behaviour in social organisations. So studies which appear to support Maslow involve us in circularity. Since his studies are based on the observation of people in social organisations and the ways in which individuals and groups build social structures to provide for their needs and desires, and since hierarchical status predicts satisfaction with needs, studies which confirm Maslow's theory by correlating satisfaction of needs with social status are engaged in the circular process of demonstrating that a theory formulated on the basis of social observation can be supported by observation of the forms of social organisation. We cannot break through to anything that would confirm that Maslow has discovered a hierarchy of motive-forces. He implied that he had discovered a hierarchy of motive-forces which interacts with the social situation in which people find themselves. Yet his hierarchy of needs, which purports to be based in biological structures, is derived solely from a social context: the needs themselves are only known from what other people are seen to do, so that the explanation is circular. Indeed this circularity is a feature of all personality and motivational perspectives where personality traits and psychological needs are treated as unseen mechanical forces that cause human behaviour.

Managers could promote Maslow's theory as a statement that they should direct their energies towards emancipating colleagues from inferior levels of need, leaving them to work as individuals towards the rather vague higher levels. If, however, we engage in everyday discourse, which assumes that individuals are selecting the ends to be achieved and choosing what is necessary for their accomplishments according to their circumstances, we must conclude that they are working with a fluid value-structure: what is vital today may be of no moment tomorrow. Maslow converts this into a fixed hierarchy, which is untenable, and admits needs as mechanical forces. I do not know whether the managers and trainers who promote his theory follow him in this policy. Given the popularity of psychometric testing, where the assumption of force is explicit, it seems likely that they do.

The debate between Drucker and Maslow was part of a wider debate between managing by performance and managing by personality. What is at issue is the role of psychology in management and the degree to which managers want to become psychologists. Drucker argued that management is a practice and that managers are judged and judge others on the basis of objective performance. Maslow argued that management is a form of the human encounter which requires psychological insight into the personality and motives of others. Maslow was not alone and had an army of motivational psychologists to support him, including David McClelland, Frederick Herzberg and other psychologists who became famous, rich and surprisingly influential in the cut-throat business of management consultancy.

One of the most successful management consultants and motivational psychologists, Harvard professor David McClelland, declared that his favourite motive – need-achievement – is the 'mental virus' which causes people to become entrepreneurs. Apparently it is the need-power virus that causes other people to become managers. Motives, according to McClelland, are learned. In *The Achieving Society*, he argued that the need to achieve is a motive which is absorbed from subtle aspects of parental training, including an emphasis on aspiration, independence, self-reliance and achievement. But what can be learned can be unlearned or forgotten, so motives and the notion of personality they support become highly volatile concepts. McClelland's concept of motive trades, like Maslow's, on human purposiveness and does not really accord with the idea of a force or trait. To pursue material success as an entrepreneur in American society is more like a reasonable choice of means to secure success than a fixed personality disposition. Furthermore, it is probable that the same people who become entrepreneurs would seek success in other walks of life, regardless of the manner in which their parents behaved towards them. There is also the problem of those brought up in the ethos prescribed for prospective entrepreneurs who become something quite different, managers for example. The idea that motives are learned compelled McClelland to deny that personality is a matter of fixed traits that cut across rational behaviour. He was obliged to demonstrate that the achievement motive is anything more than ordinary rational, purposive behaviour. To achieve this, he needed to demonstrate that this motive springs from the person in spite of the environment, and his assumption that it is learned prevented such a demonstration.

Like Maslow's theory, McClelland's theory of motivation became popular in the 1960s with managers when it was reported that they too were motivated by the achievement virus. Only later were they re-diagnosed as suffering from a power virus. Incidentally, McClelland and other 'need' theorists contravene a basic rule of English grammar, which stipulates that if a noun is used adjectivally it must precede the noun it qualifies and not the other way round. So we find McClelland describing ambition as 'need achievement' or 'n Ach' instead of achievement need; power seeking is 'need power' or 'n Pow'; sociability is 'need affiliation' or 'n Aff'. Mercifully, he doesn't commit them to a hierarchy of viruses.

Stanislav Andreski had great fun with the notion of 'need'. To prove to himself that he too could make pseudo-scientific discoveries and that his opposition to psychologists was not motivated by impotent envy, he sent a letter to a sociological journal. In his witty book, *Social Sciences as Sorcery*, he quoted a sample of his paper and invited the reader to guess what he meant by 'n Bam':

> In connection with David McClelland's article it might be relevant to report that the preliminary results of our research project into the encoding processes in communication flow indicate that (owing to their multiplex permutations) it is difficult to ascertain direct correlates of 'n Aff.' On the other hand when on the encephalogram 'dy' divided by 'dx' is less than '0' 'n Ach' attains a significantly high positive correlation with 'n Bam', notwithstanding the partially stochastic nature of the connection between these two variables.

After the publication of this letter, Andreski was approached by the managers of several industrial research organisations who offered cooperation. After inviting his readers to decipher what his letter actually said, he offered the following translation:

> Owing to the waywardness of human nature it is difficult to find out why people join a given group, but observation of how people speak and write clearly suggests that, when the brain is slowing down, a desire to achieve often gives rise to a need to bamboozle.[1]

Andreski argued that the use of the letter 'n' helps authors cash in on the prestige of mathematics, which seems to be the only reason for replacing 'desire' with 'need' or 'n'. As any rational person knows, people often desire what they do not need, and what may even do them harm (such as excessive food), while needing what they do not desire (such as constructive criticism).

Apart from Maslow and McClelland, the most influential theorist of motivation in Australian management was Frederick Herzberg who is remembered for his claim that money is not a motivator. When it was learned that, in the 1970s, he was charging thousands of dollars for a lecture and was challenged by a member of his audience to defend his theory of motivation, his legendary reply was: 'Hell, I didn't say money doesn't matter.'

In the late 1950s, Herzberg and his colleagues reviewed motivational research spanning fifty years and 28,000 employees. The most frequently mentioned sources of job satisfaction were the 'social aspects of the job', a term which the authors used to refer to all job contacts made by employees with their colleagues.

The second most frequently mentioned factor was the employees' interactions with their supervisors. But it was not social interaction in any general sense that is satisfying to an individual, but specific kinds of outcomes, such as having power over or being liked by others. Herzberg concluded that satisfied employees are realistic about their lives and goals, more flexible, better adjusted people who have the capacity to overcome the effects of poor environments. Dissatisfied employees, on the other hand, are often rigid, inflexible, unrealistic in their choice of goals, unable to overcome problems, and generally unhappy.

With his 1968 book, *Work and the Nature of Man*, Herzberg hit the management jackpot and toured the conference circuit as a guru for the next decade. In 1995 the International Press announced that this book was one of the ten most influential books in management in the twentieth century.

Herzberg began with the assumption that humans have animalistic and achievement needs. The achievement needs are like Maslow's growth needs and are concerned with the uniquely human desire to grow psychologically. The animalistic needs are concerned with the job environment and the achievement needs with the content of the job.

Herzberg noted that employees responded differently to questions about what they liked and disliked about their jobs. So he asked 200 engineers and accountants in Pittsburgh to recall 'critical incidents' when they had felt 'exceptionally good' or 'exceptionally bad' about their jobs.

He found that incidents relating to 'good' periods tended to refer to the content of the work itself, while those relating to 'bad' periods were mainly concerned with the context in which work was performed. He therefore separated 'motivating' factors which lead to job satisfaction from 'hygiene' factors which prevent dissatisfaction but do not promote satisfaction.

Factors involved in job content – achievement, recognition, challenge, responsibility and advancement – are strong de-terminants of satisfaction. Factors involved in job dissatisfac-tion, however, are rarely involved in events that led to positive job attitudes. Also, unlike the satisfiers, the dissatisfiers con-sistently produced short-term changes in job attitudes. The major dissatisfiers are company policy and administration, supervision, salary, interpersonal relationships and working conditions. Since the dissatisfiers describe the environment and serve primarily to prevent job dissatisfaction while having little effect on positive job attitudes, Herzberg named them 'hygiene' factors.

The satisfiers were named 'motivators' since they are effective in motivating people to superior effort. It would follow that the way to motivate working people is through job enrichment: challenging work for which employees assume responsibility. Herzberg noted, however, that managers usually try to bribe employees with hygiene factors, such as incentive schemes and fringe benefits. What is needed is more emphasis on good, old-fashioned Puritan virtues, notably hard work, responsibility and achievement.

Herzberg also applied his theory to the vexed field of mental health. Mental illness is not the mere absence of mental health. Nor is mental health the mere absence of mental illness. Mental health and illness are two separate dimensions representing approach behaviour (mental health) and avoidance behaviour (mental illness). Combining his interest in work motivation with mental health, he asserted that employees who seek to obtain satisfactions from material rewards (rather than from sources approved by managers) are not only 'sick', 'unhealthy' and 'maladjusted', but 'mentally ill', 'neurotic' and 'pathological' as well. He argued that satisfaction with material rewards (which may reduce deprivation) indicates emotional immaturity. Employees who are deprived in some physical or financial way are more likely to suffer emotional problems, but if the source of deprivation is removed (say by paying them more) they are still likely to have emotional problems unless they develop interests in 'higher order' factors, such as achievement, challenge and responsibility. Obviously employees at the bottom of organisational hierarchies are more likely to be denied access to challenging jobs and their concern with material rewards would seem reasonable. According to Herzberg, however, they are neurotic.

Throughout the 1970s it was a form of sport for psychologists to criticise Herzberg's theory. It is easily done. By relying on a story-telling method he is vulnerable to the charge that the differences between stated sources of satisfaction and dissatisfaction stem from defensive processes. People are more likely to attribute the causes of satisfaction to their own achievements while attributing their dissatisfaction to factors in their environment. When researchers used methods other than the critical-incident storytelling approach, Herzberg's results were not confirmed. Despite, or because of, academic criticism, Herzberg's influence on Australian management increased throughout the 1970s. His theory was appropriated by people interested in job enrichment and the semi-autonomous work group movement in Scandinavia. If managers are serious in their desire to maximise job satisfaction at the workplace, it followed from Herzberg's theory that they should eliminate sources of job dissatisfaction from the work environment and increase possibilities for job enrichment by redesigning jobs to promote personal challenge and responsibility. But Herzberg was adamant that job enrichment must be based on an 'individual' psychology of motivation (popular in America and based on a Protestant Ethic ideology) and not on the 'group' psychology (popular in Scandinavia and widely but erroneously associated with socialism).

Herzberg's comparison between individual and group psychology is crucial to an understanding of the confusions that developed in Australian management in the 1970s and led to the rejection of job enrichment programs that were based on the Scandinavian model. By the 1980s, Australian managers had, with Herzberg's help, buried the Scandinavian approach and were dancing with psychologists and consultants who were promoting Japanese ideas. Australian managers preferred Herzberg's 'individual' psychology, with its emphasis on individual achievement, personal responsibility and recognition for personal achievement, to the Scandinavian emphasis on group behaviour. These concepts are consistent with the Protestant Ethic, which is an appropriate ideology for a red-blooded American psychologist like Herzberg who simply ignored power relationships in favour of personal motives.

Herzberg argued that the European emphasis on worker participation and industrial democracy reflects the ideological bias of (democratic) socialism, while his defence of Protestant individualism reflected the ideology of American capitalism – although he did not use those words. Scandinavian psychologists, notably Bertil Gardell, argued that while managers gain their power and satisfaction from their job and higher-order motives, blue-collar workers gain their power and satisfactions through the group. Herzberg, however, feared the domination of the individual by the group and directed his attention to the virtues of individual achievement and personal recognition, which may be valid for managers but sentences blue-collar workers to impotence.

In 1974, when Herzberg was treading the boards at management conferences, David Jenkins published a critique of Herzberg and his version of job enrichment. *Job Power* had little influence on Australian managers who preferred the motivation-hygiene gospel preached by the globe-trotting missionary. Though delivered with wit and energy, Herzberg's message became increasingly shrill and dogmatic. When members of his audiences, especially Europeans, suggested that human motivation is more complex than he indicated, the guru frequently implied that research undertaken since his own had been quite unnecessary and replied: 'You got an expert's answer'. Confronted with studies which showed that when faced with boring and repetitive work, workers view high pay and good physical working conditions as the only sources of satisfaction, which is not supposed to happen according to his theory, Herzberg retreated to the position that such people are neurotic.

Herzberg's version of job enrichment yields only limited changes since the way in which the jobs are enriched is decided, not by workers, but imposed without group discussion by the external job enrichment experts, or human resource managers. He was against group action and participation in decision-making processes and was worried that workers would participate beyond their level of competence. Jenkins is surely right when he argued that Herzberg's popularity among American (and Australian) managers depended on his method's very limited objectives.

While it goes some way toward satisfying some employees, it does not alter prevailing power relationships. After all, Herzberg had said that the authoritarian pattern of American industry will continue 'despite the propaganda for a more democratic way of life.' And telling managers that money is not a motivator must have come as a pleasant surprise to those who regard wages as a cost to be minimised.

Jenkins lamented the lack of progress in job enrichment in America despite Herzberg's popularity and he asked why it should be that, after such a promising start, managers and employees had been overtaken by feelings of apathy about its prospects. The same was said of job enrichment and worker participation in Australia, by Russell Lansbury for example. In stark contrast, Scandinavian psychologists were reporting significant progress with semi-autonomous work groups in which employees were given and responded positively to increased levels of control over their jobs. Yet the degree of interest in the U.S. in job enrichment through increased job control was close to zero. Jenkins pointed out that this apathy was not confined to managers, who might be expected to resist changes in relative power structures, but was also widespread among trade union officials, social scientists and social commentators generally.

It was left to the Scandinavians to take the lead in job enrichment and to face the problems of power and authority relationships. One of the leading exponents in this area was Einar Thorsrud, whose work at Nobo Fabrikker and Norsk Hydro paved the way for 'task force' type operations in Sweden, notably at the Volvo and Saab factories. Thorsrud, with help from Australia's Fred Emery, reorganised work practices to such an extent that through the establishment of groups with common goals, power relationships were improved. Jenkins noted that it is significant that Thorsrud's basic assumptions of human motivation were similar to Herzberg's. Yet Herzberg, who was against group actions of this type, refused to confront the problems of power and authority generated by such action, such as the doubts raised by job enrichment programs about the unwarranted size of middle management. For Herzberg, each individual is to be dealt with individually.

Herzberg disapproved of the Scandinavian experiments and what he regarded as their major disadvantage: group tyranny. He was concerned about the individual and not the group member per se, assuming that individuals can be subtracted from their social milieu. He made outlandish claims about fundamental differences between theories which emphasise personal responsibility (like his) and others which do not. He argued that employee commitment to groups, far from being a source of power for them, robs them of their individuality. Not only is this not supported empirically, it is not even a feature of Scandinavian theory. Rather, it is consistent with a pervasive Protestant Ethic ideology which Herzberg scarcely bothered to conceal. When researchers compared work experiences on the production lines of Sweden and Detroit, there was no evidence that the Swedes were tyrannised by the group and considerable evidence that they were healthier, more productive and motivated to work. The wide gap between American and Scandinavian ideas about job enrichment was illuminated during a seminar at which Thorsrud and Herzberg were present. Jenkins reported that Herzberg was expressing his gloomy views on the dangers of worker participation and Thorsrud replied that he (Herzberg) was against participation for the very reasons the Scandinavians were in favour of it: one doesn't know where it will stop.

By removing the emphasis from problems of material and financial deprivation to personal inadequacies and emotional immaturity, Herzberg's theory contradicted several studies which showed that it is rational for blue-collar workers to be concerned with their physical, material and financial well-being. If managers believe that negotiating for higher wages and better working conditions is indicative of incipient madness or blatant irrationality, they are following in the footsteps of one of the most influential industrial psychologists of the twentieth century. Such a fact might be comical if it occurred only in caricature. Unfortunately, the reality is that many Australian managers believed it. One consequence was that Scandinavian experiments were routinely dismissed in the late 1970s as misguided, impractical and ideologically unsound.

There were some notable exceptions, however. A handful of companies encouraged participation and involvement by employees on the shop-floor. These programs included the election by work groups of their own supervisors, the restructuring of jobs to provide workers with greater opportunities to exercise choice and initiative, and the creation of self-managing work groups which managed their own work schedules and decided how tasks should be shared and performed. The underlying objective of these programs was to introduce 'management from below' to replace the traditional approach of 'rule from above'. Fred Emery's work with the Scandinavian industrial democracy projects influenced much local activity in this field. The introduction of semi-autonomous work groups at CSR Limited, for example, required an increase in the range of workers' skills, as was the case with the self-managing work groups in Pacific Can Company.[2]

When in 1979, I went to Sweden to work with Bertil Gardell, I was able to study at first-hand the semi-autonomous work groups at Volvo and Saab. While there, the news from Australia was that such studies were a waste of time because the heady days of 'industrial democracy', championed in Don Dunstan's state of South Australia, were over. On my return to Australia in 1980, the refrain from managers was: 'You can't transplant Sweden to Australia.' True enough, but having rejected the possibility of borrowing ideas from one country, Australian managers began their long love affair with another: Japan.

In 1982, *International Management* published a cover story headed, 'Where have all the management gurus gone?'[3] The authors noted that there were no new faces in the gallery of management gurus. Since psychologists entered the field of management in the 1950s and 1960s, there have been no writers to rival Herzberg, McGregor or Maslow. The authors conceded that of all the influential management scribes, only Drucker was still producing original and stimulating material.

Drucker himself conceded that the new management gurus were yet to be discovered. Those with the potential to achieve eminent status were busy writing books telling people how to make money out of nuclear war or how to profit from world starvation.

In the early 1980s, however, there were many Australian managers who believed that a new guru had emerged who could explain the unexplainable: the workings of the Japanese mind. William G. Ouchi joined the long list of management professors who attempted to understand the 'Japanese miracle' and educate local managers in the ways of the Japanese. At a time when Japanese productivity was the highest in the world, it is hardly surprising that American and Australian managers responded favourably to an author who offered to lead them from the halcyon days of American human relations to a new era of Japanese-style paternalism. The Japanese model promised to replace obsessions with job satisfaction and sociability with concerns for productivity and adaptation to a new era of 'consumer freedom'. The gurus of the 1950s and 1960s had, with the notable exception of Drucker, passed into history precisely because the world's economic and social developments had rendered their ideas impotent.

By the early 1980s, however, it had become obvious to many managers that concerns for and improvements to employees' levels of job satisfaction had not resulted in improvements in productivity, absenteeism or industrial conflict. Furthermore, the short-lived movement for worker participation threatened to put more power into the hands of trade unionists at a time when citizens of the developed countries were telling opinion polls that union officials should have less power. Oddly enough, union officials themselves allowed the participation movement to die without a whimper. Some in union officialdom believed that worker participation would lead to a coalition of employers and unionists against consumers at a time when consumers were demanding more freedom. Others were concerned it would compromise the power of trade unions, and even render them irrelevant. A new management guru would have to address a different set of problems and develop a radically different approach to management. Australian managers had moved into an era of discontinuity and they had to learn how to manage in turbulent times. Apart from Drucker's new books, they could no longer rely on Maslow, McClelland and Herzberg.

Then along came Ouchi, who advised managers to prepare for the new era of productivity by learning from those great producers: the Japanese. His best-selling book *Theory Z* purported to show how American managers could meet the Japanese challenge. He argued that companies which resemble the large Japanese organisations could significantly increase employee satisfaction and productivity because they were homogeneous and collectivistic and allowed individual behaviour to mesh intimately. By comparison, Ouchi argued, American organisations were heterogeneous and individualistic, which meant that people linked tenuously to one another. He brought a smile to readers when he claimed that such American organisations as IBM, Procter and Gamble, Hewlett-Packard and Eastman Kodak had adopted Japanese structures and should therefore be emulated. Acknowledging McGregor's Theory Y, Ouchi referred to these 'American/ Japanese' organisations as Type Z. As we have seen, Theory Y was more a program than a theory and McGregor used it to argue for participative management and the decentralisation of organisational power. In the early1960s this was radical thinking. By the 1970s it was all the rage, until Australian managers decided to waltz with the Japanese. And along came Ouchi to teach them how to dance.

Ouchi believes that Z organisations are based on clans rather than hierarchies. Clans succeed when teamwork replaces individual performance. And because of the relative absence of bureaucratic controls, individuals report a higher sense of personal autonomy, which makes them work with more enthusiasm than their counterparts in Western organisations. Before proceeding, a few comments about the consequences of not working with enthusiasm are in order.

While Ouchi provided a general description of the workings of Japanese society, he failed to analyse the relationship between social authority and organisational authority. Indeed the word 'authority' does not appear in his index. Rather, he followed the American tendency to explain authority relationships in terms of trust. For example, he believed that the authoritarian system of job placement in Japan, in which students from elite universities are selected for work in elite companies, is based on trust. So, for Ouchi, the first lesson of Theory Z is trust, and productivity and trust go hand in hand, 'strange as that may seem.' Not strange at all because with trust and productivity go power and authority.

And it is all too easy to explain employee obedience by an appeal to feelings of intimacy and trust and ignore the fact that the penalties for disobedience and distrust are very severe indeed. It may be that feelings of autonomy make the Japanese work enthusiastically. Alternatively, feelings of autonomy may be rationalisations which enable the Japanese to accept the limits to their autonomy which result from social conditions that support life-time employment (in the large companies and government departments) and provide significant rewards to those who conform to the system.

Ouchi acknowledged the weaknesses of the clan model: xenophobia, overweening conformity and conservatism, racism, sexism, loss of professionalism. But although Theory Z is based on trust, mutual obligation, consensus and harmony, Ouchi failed to address the crucial issues of conflict, tensions and pressures which characterise the daily life of Japanese employees and the bitter factional fighting which consume most Japanese managers. Drucker had warned his American readers that Japanese business life is a saga of unremitting guerrilla warfare.[4] Where the foreigner sees close cooperation between government and business, the Japanese managers see government bureaucrats meddling and dictating to them, a constant tug-of-war between and within organisations. In this respect, Ouchi was indeed a foreigner. He saw trust, harmony and consensus where others saw a finely balanced system of power relationships. He was right to extol the virtues of trust and intimacy, since part of the Japanese success story of the 1980s was based on the willingness of the various parties to establish areas of common concern. He was also right in pointing out that work organisations are profoundly shaped by the social environment in which they operate. But this insight was set aside when Theory Z was born. By imposing a personal model of harmony and consensus upon the Japanese experience, he misunderstood its power relationships.

Ouchi's star has faded and he is rarely mentioned today. Similarly, the glories of Japan have faded into history and managers today are more interested in understanding China and India, although they are reluctant to look to those countries for management models. Ouchi marched to the tune of those naïve psychologists who claimed that the adversarial relationships between American managers and workers should be replaced by mutual trust. He offered benevolent paternalism at a time when managers were witnessing the beginning of the end of 'organisation man'. Ouchi's brief success signalled the end of an era. Theory Z was a pendant to McGregor's psychology of 1960. He continued, and perhaps concluded, the tradition of human relations thinkers who have survived far longer than many would have predicted.

A few psychologists have argued that psychology might dispense with motive-forces and pursue alternative, scientific explanations for human conduct. This move redirects attention to finding a mechanism for choice and this has not led to an easy solution either. As long as the notion of motive-force remains in psychology, these difficulties will remain. A motive-force must take the form of a force which either originates in the person or becomes attached to some external object endowing it with positive or negative value.

The science psychologists like to emulate is Newtonian physics, which uses the concept of force successfully in explaining motion. Why, then, is it such a dismal failure in psychology? Newton's laws of motion do not provide for a category for bodies which move spontaneously, independent of external forces. The intact human body is in constant spontaneous motion while alive, even during sleep. Consequently, insofar as people move themselves, they are excluded from Newton's model, but insofar as they are moved by external forces they come within its charter. So if we take a bus, the movement of our body is amenable to physical explanations, but if we walk it is not. So far as scientific psychology has based itself on Newtonian mechanics, it looks like an attempt to extend mechanical methods of experiment and deterministic thinking to human behaviour. Clearly, the language of Newtonian mechanics is inapplicable to a psychology which emphasises freedom and responsibility.

Yet motivation remains a popular, if confused, topic in psychology. Its popularity, which it shares with personality psychology and psychoanalysis, is due to the never-ending human quest to discover the keys to the inner kingdom of the brain/mind. Its confusion turns on the ambiguity of the term and the way it can be used to describe mechanical, determined behaviour or purposive, freely chosen action. Sometimes authors of psychology books appear not to appreciate the difference, or in Maslow's case, shift from one meaning to another.

Psychology has failed to solve the problem of human motivation. Its function as a motive-force has been a failure because it turns out to be either circular or a metaphor for purpose. The main difficulty is that it cannot account for both motion and purposive action. Ethically, the idea of motive-as-cause has been useful in allowing people to deny their power or choice and personal responsibility. And if psychologists switch their allegiance to the notion of motive-as-reason, there are as many motives as there are reasons. To have a motive for all aspects of behaviour raises a very odd question. If we can describe these bits of behaviour, and to add the motive is to introduce circularity of explanation, why employ the motive construct at all?

5

THE PERSONALITY CULT

Personality: what poorly motivated people have to fall back on.

Apart from the hundreds of definitions of personality, there are thousands of personality traits to be found in a dictionary. For decades, personality psychologists have been constructing tests to measure these traits. The results are analysed statistically by factor analysis, which groups the results into clusters. Each cluster represents a number of traits which are statistically, though by no means perfectly, related to each other, such as 'active' and 'impulsive'. Psychologists frequently and acrimoniously disagree about which form of factor analysis is appropriate and what the factors should be called.

Factor analysts are normally not even expected to show that the measure provided by their factors is reliable, despite the fact that many scales derived from this procedure are anything but reliable. Since factor analysis is a technique used to reduce a large number of correlated items to a few factors which are indicative of the number of dimensions involved, one would like to believe that factor analysts could agree on the number of factors involved in personality. But they cannot. Some personality psychologists have staked their reputations on sixteen or more factors while others, notably Hans Eysenck, preferred a more parsimonious solution.

Personality traits are measured by adding individuals' answers to questions which purport to assess behavioural themes and by which individuals are compared to others in a group. Particular traits are then reduced to personality factors which are classification systems, even though they are treated as inner causes of behaviour. So a person works hard because of 'ambition' or gains the support of others because of 'sociability'. Yet all that is available by way of evidence is the behaviour from which the trait was inferred.

The popularity of personality tests suggests that psycho-managers do not regard performance as the ultimate test of management. Or, to put it another way, the traditional test of management has been compromised by psychomanagers and psychologists since personality is, according to empirical evidence spanning more than half a century, unrelated to work performance. These findings, endlessly replicated, should lead to the rational conclusion that personality tests can make no contribution to management. But the opposite, irrational conclusion, prevails.

Despite the logical and empirical problems that dominate the field, psychomanagers continue to pay psychologists to measure personality traits, and subject individuals to psycho-metric tests in the belief, or hope, that the elusive relationship between performance and personality will be found. Some psychomanagers accept the lack of relationship between personality and performance but argue that personality tests enable them to make decisions about the 'fit' between individual and organisation. But since personality and performance are unrelated, decisions about 'organisational fit' are based on prejudices, stereotypes and caricatures. One still hears psychomanagers claim that extraverts make better sales representatives than do introverts, individuals with low anxiety are more productive than those with high anxiety, high levels of emotional intelligence predict success in management, and so on. There is no empirical evidence to support any of these assumptions.

Defenders of psychometric tests have claimed that knowing something about another person's personality enables managers to do their jobs more effectively. The assumption is that since personality determines performance, managers can motivate their subordinates by reducing them to specific personality traits and applying motivational techniques thereto. But personality does not 'determine' performance, wholly or partly. Personality traits do not 'exist' in the way in which work performance 'exists'. Traits are inferences from behaviour and they do not cause behaviour. Psychomanagers are not content to work with behaviour, however. They seek the keys to the kingdom of the psyche.

Personality testers rely on evidence – personal, anecdotal, empirical – to conclude that the theory that personality predicts performance is valid. However, all empirical hypotheses are conjectural in the sense that we shall never be able to have absolute confidence that they are true, even if most of us would agree to accept some conjectures as more credible than others. While no number of black ravens could verify the claim that all are black, a single raven that is not black can falsify the hypothesis. The strength of a scientific theory, therefore, rests on its ability to withstand criticism.

The theory that personality predicts management performance has been repeatedly falsified by hundreds of studies over a period exceeding fifty years. The history of failure has been so pronounced that personality trait theory should be regarded as a degenerated research program. But that would be to underestimate the power of bad science and vested interests. Indeed, personality testing in industry and government has never been more popular. The authors of a recent textbook write:

> It appears that the use of these [personality] tests for recruitment purposes in Australian organisations is increasing, despite criticism of them as unreliable and unethical. In a recent survey of 8000 people, 44% viewed psychometric tests as too invasive with regard to personal facts and details. In contrast, 69% of HR directors who were surveyed reported that the tests are extremely valuable in the recruiting process.[1]

Personality testing is big business. Professional journals include testimonials from consultants and managers who parade their paeans proudly. Paeans are justified when these songs of joy are linked to triumphant outcomes, otherwise the songs are empty and the victory pyrrhic. Sadly, a review of the personality testing industry leads to the undeniable conclusion that the triumph is based on the widespread, but false, belief that personality test scores predict individual performance. If they did one could have no empirical objection to them, although one might still object to their use with unwilling subjects on ethical grounds. But personality test scores do not predict performance, as countless scholars have pointed out for decades.

Reviewers of personality testing repeatedly insist that improvements are needed in the reliability and validity of personality tests. The general conclusion is that improvements are needed not only in the reliability and validity of personality tests but also in their theoretical underpinnings and the criteria against which they are validated. Popular tests are invalid indicators of what they purport to measure, infringe on the individual's right to privacy, and foster unethical management practices. No surprises here since this is a familiar refrain. It is a disheartening experience to hear apologists agree that the old popular tests were unreliable and invalid, but assure us that new tests have overcome earlier problems. It is a discreditable business when psychologists tell clients that their tests can predict behaviour while admitting that there are no relevant validation studies. Which personalities are desirable and which are undesirable? We cannot know.

Personality psychologists claim that the acquisition of various skills is influenced by personality traits. This claim still awaits empirical evidence to support it. And it is difficult to see how it could ever find such support given the theoretical nature of traits and the vast discrepancy between what people say and what they do. Personality traits are abstractions so they cannot cause anyone to do anything. How then did testers convince people that personality traits exist and can be measured? Since many psychologists treat traits as 'mental forces', they needed to convince people that they are populated by invisible powers. A linguistic trick was needed and it has been prosecuted with unbelievable success.

The trick is based on the practice of turning verbs and adverbs into abstract nouns and reifying them: treating the abstract nouns as if they are concrete nouns. Concrete nouns refer to such things as tables; abstract nouns do not refer to things, which is why they are called 'abstract'. So the verb 'think' became the abstract noun 'thought', 'feel' became 'feeling', 'intelligently' became 'intelligence', 'create' became 'creativity', 'imagine' became 'imagination', 'depressed' became 'depression', and so on. If an abstract noun, say 'thought', is treated as a concrete noun, a place has to be found to house it. The house is either another abstraction called 'mind' (from the verb 'to mind'), or a concrete entity – brain – although logic demands that an abstraction cannot be located anywhere. In this way people are populated with abstractions, including thoughts, feelings, values, intelligences and minds. While it is true that we think, feel, value, act intelligently (sometimes), and mind (as in 'mind the step'), it is not true that we have 'things' called thoughts, feelings, values, intelligences or minds.

Reifying abstract nouns allows management performance to be explained by 'pride' or 'ambition' although it is impossible to determine which trait is the cause of performance. Used thus, reification is a powerful political tool because it enables psychomanagers to identify people whose personalities don't 'fit' or who lack a 'well-rounded personality'. In extreme cases, it enables them to conclude that their colleagues are suffering from a 'personality disorder'.

Furthermore, the study of personality traits is based on tautology. When we are told that a person acts from a trait which, at the time of acting, is the dominant one, we are in the grip of tautology. Traits cannot be observed, so they are inferred from observations of behaviour, including answers to test questions. Aggression is an inference from the observation that a particular person frequently acts aggressively. The circularity of reasoning is obvious. How do we know that a person has a trait called 'aggression'? He has a trait called 'aggression' because he acts aggressively. Why does he act aggressively? He acts aggressively because he has a trait called 'aggression', or an 'aggressive personality'.

It is axiomatic that when we make a claim of the form x (aggression) causes y (aggressive behaviour), x and y must be separately identifiable. We can identify aggressive behaviour (y) but no one has ever observed a personality trait called 'aggression' (x). So when we are told that a person acts from the trait which, at the time of acting, is the dominant one, the statement is tautological. It is logically impossible that a person could 'possess' a dominant trait and yet be driven into action by a subordinate trait. If the subordinate trait is 'causing' the behaviour, it is by definition the dominant trait. Personality trait psychology, therefore, is based on a tautology. And from a tautology one cannot deduce a statement about the empirical world: tautologies have only tautological consequences. One cannot, for example, deduce from the tautology 'what will be, will be', that effort is worthless. Similarly, one cannot deduce from the tautology that one acts from a dominant trait that there are any such traits. Personality trait psychology is trapped in circularity.

There is an escape route for those who want to assess behavioural trends but do not wish to populate the individual with personality traits. Answers to personality tests can be treated as communications about the hypothetical situations invented by test designers, including the testing environment itself. Needless to say, the logic of the testing situation is conveniently ignored by testers who assume that subjects answer questionnaire items honestly and thereby reveal something about their habitual patterns of behaviour. Testers assume that measured patterns of behaviour are triggered by social situations similar to those described in questionnaires. This chain of reasoning is weak at every link. Behaviour, as everyone knows, varies according to the situation in which one finds oneself. The results of personality tests are communications not traits, self-reports not needs, and they are particularly responsive to the demands of one's social situation.

Psychologists cannot know another person's inner experiences: all they can know are communications about them. Personality tests cannot measure inner experiences: they measure honest and dishonest communications. Since many people are required to undergo personality testing against their will, some communicate dishonestly. Indeed, faking personality tests is so widespread and so easy to accomplish that it is surprising that the results are taken seriously. There have been numerous demonstrations that faking can be successful. And the claim that personality tests contain lie scales which can identify fakers is risible. In *The Organization Man*, William Whyte made fools of personality testers when he wrote an appendix: 'How to Cheat on Personality Tests'. Legions of people followed his sensible advice.

After reviewing more than half a century's research on personality testing, many scholars have concluded that they cannot under any circumstance advocate the use of personality tests as a basis for making decisions about individual performance. Faced with low validity data, advocates have blamed the adverse results on poor research practices and have used statistical sleight of hand to convince a gullible public of the importance of personality tests. The technical deficiencies of the most widely-used tests are well known. For example, the Humm-Wadsworth Temperament Scale (HWS) has poor reliabilities, which raises concerns about the accuracy of individual assessments. The popular Myers-Briggs Temperament Indicator (MBTI) contradicts the original Jungian ideas on which it is based and studies using the test have neither confirmed the theory nor validated the measure.

Developed in the U.S. in the early 1930s, the HWS was known in the 1940s as a 'people-sorting instrument'. 'People-sorters' were early personality tests designed to meet the needs of big business. And they, in turn, became big business. 'People-sorters' first became popular in the 1920s when they were used for dubious purposes, such as screening out political liberals and union sympathisers. In *The Servants of Power*, Loren Baritz reported that the HWS was used at Lockheed to identify and remove possible troublemakers from among employment applicants. Another company used personality tests to discover whether applicants' wives dominated their family decisions, because it was believed that such men would be easy to manage and this was just the sort of men the company wanted. The HWS was used to detect such temperaments as autistic, paranoid, epileptoid, depressive, manic, hysteroid, schizoid and cycloid. 'Normal-cycloid' individuals are, it seems, good salespeople while 'normal-autistics' are good accountants. It was assumed that every job had an ideal personality to 'fit' it. The challenge was to find the right cog for the machine.

Isabel Myers, a Philadelphia housewife, read about the HWS in a 1942 *Reader's Digest* and decided to enter the people-sorting business to make people nicer. Inspired by an eccentric reading of Carl Jung, Myers developed the MBTI which assesses the extent to which individuals have a dominant preference for particular behaviours and ways of thinking. A self-report, forced-choice test, its four 'preference' scales measure extraversion-introversion, sensing-intuiting, thinking- feeling, judging-perceiving. Because of the method of scoring (based on dichotomies) there have been legitimate concerns about the test's psychometric properties and its use in business and academic environments. Several researchers have failed to replicate the MBTI's factor structure and concluded that the naming of the factors is vague and tendentious. Sound empirical investigations of the test are rare and it has been difficult to establish relationships between personality types and organisational factors. It should not be used to 'type' individuals for particular jobs, although it has been used for that purpose. The test contains many transparent items so that it is easily faked.

The MBTI has achieved true cult status. It is now the world's most popular test according to its guardians: more than 2.5 million people take the test in a year. The MBTI is used by 89 of the Fortune 100 companies to 'identify strengths' and 'facilitate teamwork'. In *The Cult of Personality*, Annie Murphy Paul observes that, that the MBTI has also been embraced by numerous lost souls who experience a revelation upon learning about their psychological type. Their enthusiasm persists despite research showing that as many as three-quarters of testees achieve a different personality type when tested again, and the sixteen types described by the MBTI have no scientific basis whatsoever. The MBTI's positive tone blends seamlessly with the language of managerial political correctness.

It is easy to see why it appeals to so many people in management, academia, education, counselling and coaching. New age fantasists, lost souls in search of gurus or themselves, narcissists, politically correct relativists, psychologists and their clients who emphasise 'feeling and caring' rather than 'thinking and arguing', have found the MBTI a revelation.

The idea that an individual's personality should 'fit' a particular job can be seen as an attempt to shift responsibility from performance to a lack of balance between employee and management. When things go wrong, it is a lack of 'fit' that is the culprit. Since managers cannot be expected to accommodate their colleagues' developing abilities, personality distracts them from issues of job design and enrichment.

After World War II the personality testing business boomed. Cattell's 16 Personality Factor Questionnaire and many other personality tests competed for managers' purses. But psychologists could not agree on the number of personality traits that effectively summarise a personality. H.J. Eysenck said two and then three. Raymond Cattell said 16, but they were reducible to four. Then, for some quaint reason, American psychologists voted for five, claiming with the fervour of true believers, that the 18,000 traits found in a good dictionary can be reduced to the Big Five: extraversion, agreeableness, conscientiousness, emotional stability (not included in the MBTI), and openness to experience.

In 1968, Walter Mischel published *Personality and Assessment*, which had a devastating effect on the collective conscience of personality psychologists. Mischel showed that 'personality' and 'behaviour' are often used interchangeably. But whereas behaviour consists of observable events, personality is an abstraction inferred from behaviour. Clearly, 'trait' is used in a variety of ways: to refer to the differences between the observed behaviour of two or more individuals, and as a personality construct invented for its explanatory power but which does not have any concrete existence as a 'thing' or 'process' within a person. And yet many psychologists have treated traits as if they are processes that exist in persons. Moreover, traits have been treated as *causes* of behaviour when it is clear that abstractions cannot have causal power. Personality psychologists claim that because individuals respond differently to environmental stimuli, personality traits, some of which are supposed to be inherited, must be invoked as an explanation. Therefore, they claim that personality traits can and should be measured to predict individual behaviour even though research studies consistently invalidate this claim.

Mischel argued that the massive attention to personality traits has been accompanied by an equally massive neglect of environmental factors. Unless the environment changes significantly, past behaviour rather than personality test scores remains the best predictor of future behaviour in similar situations. Personality psychologists infer enduring generalised attributes in persons and attempt to predict from the inferred trait to behaviour in various situations. This would be an appropriate procedure if it could be done reliably and provided predictive power. But, Mischel argued, more than five decades of research have shown conclusively that it cannot. He concluded that traits are excessively crude concepts to encompass adequately the subtlety of human behaviour.

According to Annie Murphy Paul, the years following the publication of Mischel's book are universally described as 'dark' ones for the field of personality testing. Personality psychology was 'mired in Mischellian mud'. But it didn't take long to exchange one mud bath for another. After acknowledging the influence of social conditioning, which they had never denied, personality psychologists sallied forth under the banner of interactionism. Unfortunately, the environmentalists of the 1960s were losing ground to the biological reductionists of the

1980s, and when the Big Five taxonomy was revived Mischel's work was consigned to history.

During the 1990s there were several meta-analyses which investigated the relationship between the five magic bullets and work performance. Meta-analysis, which became very popular in the 1980s, combines the published findings of several studies in a similar field and weights them insofar as it is possible on the basis of relevant data. Inevitably, researchers disagree about many aspects of this procedure and there is much room for 'creative' interpretation. One rule is clear (or should be): meta-analytical researchers of the Big Five should not include in their data studies that use measures other than those that measure the Big Five. But this is exactly what they did. And so the results of the rival reviews differed quite significantly, spawning a public controversy as authors challenged each other's professional competence. While later meta-analyses have addressed these basic methodological issues, the findings are meagre.

Meta-analyses rely on the correlation coefficient which measures the relationship between two variables. If we want to measure how much information about the value of Y can be obtained from a knowledge of the corresponding value of X, we measure the degree of correlation between X and Y. When there is some degree of correlation between X and Y, then information about an X value contains some information about the corresponding Y value. The value of the correlation coefficient ranges from –1 through 0 to +1. When an individual has the same rank on X and Y, the correlation is perfect and has a value of +1. When a correlation is positive but less than perfect, low scores on X are associated imperfectly with low scores on Y. When X and Y are unrelated, the correlation coefficient is 0.

In connection with any quantity which varies, such as job performance, the variation does not arise solely because of differences among personalities. So the correlation coefficient is used as an indicator of the proportion of the variation in job performance, which is related to personality scores. The correlation thus provides an answer to the question: how much does the variation in personality contribute to the variation in job performance? This question may be answered in terms of variance. The square of the correlation coefficient indicates the proportion of variation in job performance, which is accounted for by differences in personality scores. If the correlation between job performance and personality scores is +.9 then the proportion of variance accounted for is 81% (and 19% is unaccounted for) and personality would be a very strong predictor of job performance. For 50% of the variance of job performance to be accounted for by personality, a correlation coefficient of just over +.7 is required. Since important employment decisions are based on the assumption that personality scores predict job performance, one would expect and hope that the correlation coefficients are greater than +.7 otherwise decision makers will make a large number of rejecting and accepting errors.

What have the meta-analyses found? Four meta-analytic studies of the relationship between job performance and personality scores yielded the following average correlation coefficients: conscientiousness .21; neuroticism .15;

extraversion .13; agreeableness .13; openness to experience .12. These results are worrying enough since the much-quoted result of .21 for conscientiousness means that the proportion of variance unaccounted for is 95.6%. Responsible decisions about hiring, promotion or training cannot be made on the basis of these figures.

However, the actual situation is far worse since it makes an important difference to the results when personality scores are correlated with 'hard' or 'soft' performance criteria. Soft criteria include subjective ratings whereas hard criteria include productivity data, salary, turnover/tenure, change of status. Since personality scores are better predictors of subjective performance ratings than objective performance measures, it is reasonable to conclude that raters rely on personality when evaluating job performance, thereby raising the question whether the relationship between personality and performance is the result of the bias of the rater rather than actual performance. In the much-quoted study by Barrick and Mount, the correlation coefficient dropped from .26 for soft criteria to .14 for hard criteria. The average correlation between the Big Five and job performance (hard criteria) was .07.[2]

These results confirm the standing joke which has dominated this industry for more than fifty years: personality testing is the '.2 industry', meaning that the proportion of variance accounted for between personality and job performance is at best 4%. Yet, neither invalid logic nor lack of scientific evidence bothers testers. Nor do the findings, suitably researched and published in respectable journals, that personality tests are discriminatory, unreliable, invalid, easily faked, and cannot predict job performance though they are used for that purpose. Since personality test scores are unrelated to management performance, there is no way to determine 'fit' with the corporate culture, and so 'fit' must be determined by other, often unstated criteria, such as getting on with the boss. Sadly, in our postmodern, politically correct, new age world of business, disagreeing with the boss, or indeed anyone, is likely to get one into trouble. People who argue with their managers are likely to be accused of low emotional intelligence and subjected to personality tests, counselling and further invasions of their privacy.

One American who was not prepared to tolerate such an invasion of privacy took the matter to court. In *Soroka v. Dayton Hudson Corporation*, a job applicant at Target Stores was required to undertake a psychological test – Psychscreen – which Target used to reject applicants who were 'emotionally unstable'.[3] Karen Grabow, a Target executive, said that she would not expect to see the calibre of the workforce improve as a result of the test but would expect that it might identify 'lunatics'. In 1989, Soroka filed a charge that use of Psychscreen discriminated on the basis of sex and religion, which are not related to work performance. Target's lawyers argued that these items could identify emotionally unstable individuals. (Question: Are people who believe in the devil emotionally unstable given that the majority of Americans believe in the devil? How would Psychscreen be scored in Australia where very few people believe in the devil?) A California court found that Target had failed to demonstrate a job-related purpose connected with Psychscreen's religious and sex items. Target appealed and in 1992 the California Supreme Court agreed to hear the case. But while Soroka waited, new legislation took effect which affected his case. The Americans with Disabilities Act of 1990 (ADA) prohibited job discrimination against a qualified individual because of a disability. The ADA required that pre-employment medical examinations be related to the relevant job. Would this include a personality test? Soroka believed it would since it is perceived as a medical examination. If so, the court could find that the use of a personality test violated the ADA. In 1993, Target executives agreed to settle without admitting liability. Target placed $1.3 million in a fund to be divided among those who had taken Psychscreen.

In *Wilson v.Johnson & Johnson* (2009), the plaintiff sued his former employer for irreparable damages that resulted from the over-use of personality tests. The jurors agreed that excessive testing caused psychological strain and led to unnecessary scrutiny resulting in personal grief. Wilson was awarded $US4.7 million.

In Australia in the late 1970s, an employee of the Commonwealth Bank left the surf on a weekend and died of a heart attack. He worked as a branch accountant and was highly regarded as a conscientious and hard-working manager. His widow sought legal advice and was told that as there was no underlying physical condition which his job could be said to have exacerbated or accelerated, she had no case at law. However, later advice suggested that it could be argued that Mr Ryan had an existing *psychological* condition which predisposed him to heart attack, especially when under stress. Mrs. Ryan, therefore, initiated legal action and in the case of *Ryan versus the Commonwealth Banking Corporation* (1978), compensation was granted. Death was found to be sufficiently related to a stressful work situation to support a finding in favour of the widow.[4]

In such cases claimants do not have to establish clear causal connections between work and illness in a way that would satisfy scientists. One of the most difficult areas of legal thought is that involving the formalisation of theories of adequate or sufficient causation. Different results may flow from the manner of approach adopted by counsel or judge.

Cases such as these raise the question of the extent to which personality factors play a part in employees' responses to stress and challenging work situations. Importantly, it raises the question as to whether such personality traits as Types A (tendency to early heart attack and stroke) and C (tendency to cancer) should be considered as predisposing factors in law. Traditionally, a predisposing, underlying condition meant a physical condition. After *Ryan versus the Commonwealth Banking Corporation* it was widely believed that underlying psychological conditions must be considered in compensation claims.

It is a lamentable fact that personality psychologists claim to know about personality but cannot agree among themselves on fundamental issues. At least 200 competing definitions are available to the perplexed student of personality, most of them so vague as to be worthless. The only theme which can be extracted from the less ambiguous definitions is that personality is known through the observation of relatively *consistent tendencies* in people's behaviour. These are referred to internal unobservable traits which are conceived of as exerting control over their conduct and thereby constituting an explanation of it.

A large part of the consistency in behaviour can be explained by the performance of roles. We expect comedians to be funny and undertakers to be serious. When we see these people acting in these ways we do not invoke personality as an explanation because they are 'in role'. In the same way, when we observe an actor playing Hamlet we do not attribute his emotional outbursts to his 'disordered personality'. What we observe in role behaviour is the application of learned skills, and their acquisition demands a certain degree of intelligence on the part of the role-player.

Human beings are also habitual creatures. We usually regard regularities in behaviour (cleaning our teeth) as purposive acts which have become relatively automatic because they are effective in achieving our goals.

Habits and role-playing are not normally attributed to personality traits because the behaviour is effective in achieving goals. But if behaviour is ineffective, if the comedian is serious and the undertaker funny, personality traits are often invoked to explain the failure to display appropriate skills.

Then there is consistent behaviour which is effective in some situations and ineffective in others. This implies a degree of rigidity which ignores the different requirements of varying situations. Again, personality traits are often invoked to explain this rigidity.

Consistency of behaviour, therefore, is not a sufficient condition for the inference of personality traits, because consistent behaviour associated with roles and habits is a rational means of achieving goals. Where people are ignorant of the behaviour needed to achieve their goals, their ineffective behaviour is not a sufficient condition for the inference of personality traits. So personality traits may be invoked when behaviour is consistent over situations in which it is ineffective, but is not due to ignorance. It follows that the only behaviour which may be held to require personality traits is that which implies a *lack of adaptability*. This is in accord with the stable character of personality traits.

Since adaptability and the capacity to acquire skills are closely related to intelligence, personality is, by definition, *negatively related to intelligence*. So personality traits constitute whatever it is that reduces the flexibility of our behaviour and makes us unable to act intelligently. For example, 'freedom' and 'responsibility' cannot meaningfully be regarded as personality traits; if anything they are anti-traits since they assume adaptability and intelligence. Yet personality psychologists not only regard them as traits but provide tests to measure them. Of course, psychologists can respond to this logic by denying that personality involves consistency of behaviour and shift to a definition which states that everything a person does, whether consistent or inconsistent, intelligent or dull, is indicative of personality. There is no escape from such a circle.

What, then, are we to make of emotional intelligence? If the advocates of emotional intelligence believe that one should express one's emotions intelligently, it is difficult to disagree with them. It is, however, easy to disagree with the widely accepted view that emotional intelligence is a personality trait. If so, it is negatively related to (cognitive) intelligence: it is *unintelligent intelligence.*

6

UNINTELLIGENT INTELLIGENCE

Intelligence tests: politically correct way of dividing them from us; bag of tricks invented by psychologists and used by managers to assess entry into their profession, but excludes nobody.

A newly minted manager received the following letter:

Dear Colleague,

Congratulations. You have been selected from a large number of candidates to attend our Advanced Management Conference to be held at the Easyrest Resort.

Your management have, with the help of highly qualified consultants, designed this year's conference to maximise your management potential so that, going forward, you can progress. Our consultants will talk to you about motivation, communication, team-building and emotional intelligence and there will be many opportunities for you to share your feelings with each other. We in senior management believe that it is important to develop a well-rounded personality and strong team spirit so that all may blend into our corporate culture. We value understanding each other, helping each other in difficult times and working together as a happy and motivated team. We believe in a management style that is people-oriented so that a collective need for achievement may emerge.

Your performance at the conference will not be rated. We are vitally interested in your potential. Our consultants will help us identify those of you who have the potential to progress in the company. Please remember to be yourself and you will get the most from this experience, going forward. My colleagues in senior management congratulate you on your selection and wish you well during your challenging course.

Yours affectionately,

Director of Human Resources, Leadership and Learning.

The recipient of this letter was an engineer in his late 30s who had been told that his career path would take him out of engineering and into management. Accordingly, he was 'invited' to the five-day management course announced in the letter. Like a lamb to the slaughter he delivered himself into the hands of three 'facilitators', ('lecturer' is an authoritarian term in the postmodern world), who told the reluctant participants to stop thinking logically (like engineers) and express their feelings. The purpose of the course was to enable the engineers and accountants to get in touch with their feelings and thereby increase their emotional intelligence. Whenever the engineer attempted to debate with the facilitators, he was forcibly reminded that his behaviour betrayed emotional insensitivity. When he asked what emotional intelligence had to do with management he was told: everything!

The concept of intelligence has had a wonderfully controversial history in psychology. It started with French government bureaucrats believing that some children were too dull to benefit from their fine schools. They decided that a short test was needed to separate those having the ability to glorify the schools from the unfortunates who did not. The test was invented by one of France's most respected psychologists, Alfred Binet, who invented tests of cognitive abilities and formed them into a scale for schoolchildren. Since cognitive ability increases with age, norms were obtained for different ages and individuals' scores related to the distribution for their age. Later, psychologists divided the 'mental age' by the chronological age to obtain a ratio called the 'intelligence quotient' or IQ. The Binet test was revised at Stanford University (in 1916) and this version was adopted by American psychologists for at least twenty years thereafter. Testing was also used during World War I to exclude the retarded from the U.S. military forces.

Psychologists were quick to see that this type of test had the potential for practical applications and, accordingly, intelligence test-making became a dominating preoccupation of psychologists. The construction of these tests depended on the use of statistical techniques of correlation. The aim was to select a number of different problems for their power to tap a similar type of ability and then graduate them according to difficulty. Items which failed to meet these criteria were discarded since they did not tap the same kind of ability. And so separate tests – such as numeracy, vocabulary and pattern perception– were produced, the scores added and the total converted by standardising against age norms.

To the surprise of psychologists it was found that the scales which had been purified so as to be scales of separate abilities always correlated positively with one another. While the correlations were not high, they were never negative. This led English psychologist Charles Spearman to invent a mathematical method of extracting what was common to groups of tests. Factor analysis produced a large common factor, which he called g (for general intelligence) and a smaller specific factor for each test. Spearman used the result to propound a two-factor theory of intelligence, each performance being held to consist of an element of general intelligence and a task-specific element. In Chicago, L. Thurstone promoted five factors that were more involved than others in successful cognitive performances and named them 'primary mental abilities'.

The disagreement between Spearman and Thurstone generated a heated debate. The Americans were offended by Spearman's theory. It was suggested that the different results arose from cultural biases, in that English society was constructed on a framework of class divisions, so that the English regarded generalists as having the higher class of intellect. Americans, on the other hand, regarded their society as more democratic and promoted a theory which did not elevate one type of intellect above all others. What seems more likely is that the difference arose from the difficulty of arriving at a rapprochement between mathematical and verbal skills.

American psychologists have consistently promoted a multi- factor definition of intelligence as can be seen in the popular book by Stephen Jay Gould, *The Mismeasure of Man*. In the 1990s, an American psychologist toured Australia arguing for seven separate intelligences. His rationale was that if teachers are encouraged to view the notion of intelligence in this way they will be less likely to downgrade students who show weakness in one area, but will try to locate their possible strengths in other areas.

In the early decades of the twentieth century Cyril Burt argued that inheritance was a strong influence in intelligence, but this idea has never been popular in the U.S. and long after Burt's death American psychologists claimed that he had fudged his data to favour his theory. While the circumstantial evidence supports this accusation, falsifying one set of scientific results is not sufficient to invalidate the theory that heredity is a factor. Numerous other studies, including some very extensive American work, suggest that it is important. But how important heredity is cannot be stated categorically. The usual ambit of positive claims is around 60% to heredity against 40% to environment. As heredity and environment interact, intelligent parents often have intelligent children, but almost always the children of intelligent parents get the best environment to grow in. So also do parents lacking in intelligence tend to have children with similar failings, but also tend to provide a less adequate educational environment.

Teachers are employed to teach, of course. Teaching is often hard work, so to keep up their own spirits and fortify themselves against the ravages of despair they are inclined to trumpet the doctrine of environmental predominance. They have to do so in order to support the basic rationale of their profession. But it is still the case, after a century of striving among educationalists and psychologists, and many optimistic claims for remedial regimes, that it has been found impossible to educate some sections of the child population beyond certain limits. (Today many teachers attribute this failure to ADHD which is treated with Ritalin).

The debate about intelligence testing became even more acrimonious when numerous research reports purported to show that the average IQ among black Americans was lower than that among white Americans. Among those who accepted these measurements as valid, this has been seen as: (a) providing a reason why whites and blacks should be treated differently; or (b) providing a justification for the existing differences in treatment. Of course the fact of a difference in IQ (if fact there is) carries no such implications at all. It is the same kind of statement as an engineer might make in comparing the relative strengths of two metals. Questions of different treatments arise only when they are considered as factors involved in something we want to achieve. But it is easy to take up the false implication; so easy that the case of the black Americans' IQ has aroused great passion. One reaction has been to impugn the validity of IQ tests. Properly constructed tests, it has been claimed, would show the black Americans to be the intellectual equal of white Americans and therefore entitled to equal treatment. This last implication is just as invalid as the original. Whether people are equal or not has no logical connection with whether they should be treated as equal. The latter is a moral choice and if it were logically tied to the actual status of equality we would be hard put to find any two people entitled to equal treatment.

Of the same family of errors is a tendency found among some feminists who point out that females (on average) are equal in IQ to males. Therefore, they argue, they are entitled to the same range of positions in the economic system as males. There is, of course, no logical connection. We may take it as a fact that the average IQ among females does not differ from that among males. Yet this does not bind us to any choice, moral or other, as to how they should spend their lives. Only if we hold to some principle that all people of equal IQ should be of equal rank in the economic system does the fact of equal IQs become pertinent.

These examples contain an element of farce, so we are inclined to say that those who make such errors are merely individuals whose discussion shows little academic merit. Surely, we think, such superficial problems cannot spell decay and death for psychology. But they are in fact very threatening, for such crusades foster the belief that what we are concerned with is reforming society by making choices which eliminate moral problems as they arise. People have been doing this for centuries with methods like preaching, propaganda, legal enforcement, appeals to emotion, bullying, even war, all of which pre-date scientific psychology and all of which can successfully change things as intended. But they do more. Changes reverberate through society and result in a whole complex of unintended effects, so that society becomes a different system, which suffers from new problems.

A case in point is the widespread belief that intelligence tests are incomplete measures of the 'total personality' because they ignore emotional skills, even though most personality tests measure emotionality/anxiety/neuroticism. In the 1990s, it was fashionable to suggest that cognitive intelligence is only half as important as 'emotional intelligence'. This gave rise to numerous tests of 'emotional intelligence' and the problems of reliability and validity arose again.

It has to be admitted that the reliability and validity of the measurement of intelligence hoped for by psychologists has proved elusive, but not so elusive that measurement is useless. One thing that disagreement about the measurement of this abstract property has stimulated is a good deal of thinking about the nature of intelligence.

'Intelligence' is an abstract noun which describes a particular relationship. One acts intelligently; one does not have intelligence. Intelligence, therefore, is an ability (or collection of abilities) which manifests itself in interactions between individuals and their environment. Unlike other species of animals, human beings can not only survive in almost any natural environment but invent novel ways of coping if the environment changes. The facts of evolution tell us that this extreme spread of capabilities must be seen as the distinguishing feature of human intelligence. Central to it is the quality of *versatility*.

If versatility is at the heart of intelligence, it is unlikely that it can be measured with the kind of precision required by the canons of science, or that we would ever need to. IQ tests were always intended to be short samples of problem-solving ability that would give a useful indication of those likely to fail, or be very slow, at learning the kinds of skills required in Western-style education. They do this quite well and it is surely unnecessary to demand that they should measure some highly abstract concept like intelligence.

In the course of schooling students steadily develop in intelligence by learning the meanings of scores of abstract names for relationships – hate, love, enmity, desire, dominance, submission, friendship, romance, competition, cooperation – and their meaning will be distinguished by the actions which are observed to identify them and the feelings which accompany them. Some of these play very important parts in workplace relationships. It comes as no surprise, therefore, to read books whose authors state the obvious: to become mature individuals we need to be knowledgeable of and versatile with respect to our emotions: we need emotional skills. If intelligence (in any form) is synonymous with versatility, then we will make a grave error to treat emotional intelligence as a personality trait. But that is exactly what the emotional intelligence movement does.

The history of the emotional intelligence movement is easily summarised, even if there is little agreement within the movement about definitions, measures and outcomes. This is a familiar story to anyone who has flirted with personality psychologists or consulted the personality trait literature.

Emotional intelligence, or the ability to emote effectively, is as old as Western philosophy. The Stoics, for example, believed that one should live one's life rationally in agreement with nature. While individuals are restricted by nature and society in many ways, they are nonetheless free to choose their emotions. They believed that rational individuals will choose to free themselves from worldly demands, negative emotions and excessive pleasure-seeking. Of three possible life-styles – the contemplative, the practical and the rational – the Stoics argued for the latter because, while human beings have been created for contemplation and action, the universe is governed by reason and fate and individuals of character exercise their reason and calmly accept their fate. Individuals of character do not allow themselves to fall victim to such self-defeating emotions as hostility, depression or anxiety. One should live in accordance with the plan of reality which can be comprehended by reason and make one's desires identical with that plan. Fools try to impose their own ideas upon reality and come to grief. Unhappiness is the result of allowing one's egoism to flout the dictates of reason and reality. One should not wish for desires: one should desire what one gets. Epictetus, for example, argued that people upset themselves not by things but by their view of them. He invited his readers to inspect their powers of reason for in these lie their abilities to control their passions. He did not suggest that one should be passionless, like a statue. Rather, he encouraged people to cultivate self-promoting emotions which help them maintain satisfactory social relations.

Stoic philosophy appears in modern psychotherapy under the banner of Rational-Emotive Behaviour Therapy (REBT), invented New York psychologist Albert Ellis. In *Reason and Emotion in Psychotherapy* he argues that emotional problems are actually psychological problems about practical problems.

In other words, motivation is a self-promoting response and distress is a self-defeating response to stress. Self-promoting responses to stress include appropriate negative feelings (concern, annoyance, sorrow, regret, frustration, disappointment). These feelings are appropriate, or rational, responses to practical problems because they are motivating, that is, they help individuals solve their practical problems. It is inappropriate, however, to respond to practical problems with feelings of anxiety, hostility or depression because these feelings sabotage effective problem solving. Rational, negative feelings are motivating; irrational negative feelings are not. Anxiety (unlike concern or determination), hostility (unlike frustration or irritation), depression (unlike disappointment or regret), sabotage practical problem solving.

As irrational feelings are related to irrational self-talk, the solution to replacing them with rational feelings turns on the ability to change one's self-talk by challenging and eliminating self-defeating beliefs. Thus, to cope with distress individuals require a rational philosophy of living.

In 1982, the American Psychological Association ranked Ellis ahead of Freud and behind Carl Rogers as the second most influential psychotherapist of the twentieth century. In a similar survey published in 2007, he was rated sixth.

Very few Australians had heard of Ellis until 1979 when Michael Bernard and I sponsored a lecture tour to Melbourne and Sydney respectively. His approach to the psychology of emotional well-being was so popular that his lectures were sold out. He was even featured on the front page of a Sydney morning newspaper because of the spectacle, witnessed by bemused reporters, of several hundred managers standing and singing lyrics composed by Ellis and set to famous operatic arias. As Ellis regarded neurosis as a fancy word for whining, he encouraged his audience to sing: 'Life really owes me the things that I miss, fate has to grant me eternal bliss, and since I must settle for less than this, whine, whine, whine!'

To understand REBT, it is useful to consider one of the specific techniques used to counteract an irrational belief about achievement. For example, those who want to achieve a goal and feel disappointed and irritated when they fail to do so are responding rationally. However, those who *demand* that they achieve a goal and feel enraged or despairing when they fail to do so are responding irrationally. It is important to note that healthy feelings of disappointment and irritation are quite different from a childish refusal to accept a world with frustrations and imperfections.

In the case of, say, a failed promotion a manager can choose to respond rationally or irrationally. There is an Activating Event (A) (news of failed promotion). The manager tells himself: 'It is unfortunate (or frustrating or disappointing) that I did not get this promotion.' This self-talk constitutes the Belief (B). Since the belief can be confirmed empirically it is a Rational Belief (rB). The Emotional Consequence (rC) is one of regret or disappointment. Unhealthy, irrational feelings, however, result from the refusal to accept the world as a place where loss or disappointments occur. Thus, there is an Activating Event (A) followed by the manager telling himself that it is *awful* or *catastrophic* that he failed to gain a promotion. The terms 'awful' and 'catastrophic', when used in this context, mean more than unfortunate or disappointing and since they have a surplus meaning, which is not empirically supportable, they constitute an Irrational Belief (iB). This results in a radically different kind of Emotional Consequence ranging from mild to extreme upset (iC).

In his early books Ellis listed ten major irrational, self-defeating beliefs which lead to poor performance and emotional upset. Modifying the original irrational ideas for managers, they are:

1. I need the approval of my superiors, subordinates and peers for everything I do.
2. I must be competent in all aspects of my work if I'm to be considered worthy.
3. Certain things my work colleagues say and do are unbearable: they should not be that way.
4. It is terrible when things go wrong at work or are not the way I want them to be.
5. When things go wrong at work I can't help but get very angry or upset.
6. I worry about aspects of my work that are threatening, difficult and challenging.
7. I need someone stronger than myself on whom I can rely when making decisions and taking business risks.
8. Many difficulties I have on the job today are due to past experiences and these problems will be with me indefinitely.
9. It is easier to avoid than to face my responsibilities.
10. There is invariably a right solution to work problems and it is terrible if this solution is not found.

Underlying these irrational beliefs are three key words: demanding, awfulising and damnation. People *demand* that they, others and the world *must* be a certain way and if they are not, they conclude that this is *awful, terrible* and *traumatic* and they *can't stand it,* so they *damn* themselves for their behaviour or they damn others and the world for its condition. There is no valid reason why we should make such demands, no valid reason for exaggerating the consequences of our 'musturbating', no valid reason for damning ourselves or others. If we aim to maximise our happiness and minimise pain, it is rational to act in a self-promoting manner and forsake irrational demands, reject emotional exaggerations and histrionics, and stop treating oneself and others as damnable beings.

In the 1970s Ellis teamed up with his friend Milton Blum to apply his psychotherapeutic theories and practices to managers. In the book he subsequently wrote for managers, *Executive Leadership: A Rational Approach,* Ellis argues that REBT can help managers enhance decisiveness, increase efficient concentration, improve relations with others, achieve self-discipline, create self-acceptance, overcome feelings of hostility, conquer depression and attack and defeat all emotional upsets.

REBT was widely embraced by Australian managers in the 1980s. Its robust, argumentative approach to problems in living and working appealed to those individuals who enjoyed confronting 'the tyranny of the shoulds'. Males responded more positively to REBT than did females who found the confrontational relationship less to their liking. Females preferred the non-confrontational, client-centred approach of Carl Rogers. As the years rolled by and Australian management became increasingly feminised, especially in HR departments, confrontational psychologies lost ground to non-directive approaches: managers were encouraged to express their feelings rather than argue with their colleagues. Rogers had his revenge on Ellis.

After reading the Stoics and Ellis it is difficult to understand why emotional intelligence was considered to be either new or interesting. Then one realises that the ancient philosophers' emphasis on rationality and freewill was unacceptable to personality psychologists who were committed to the deterministic view that emotions are not chosen but are part of one's personality structure. This is frankly acknowledged by the promoters of emotional intelligence who claim that the only assumption that the numerous and contradictory definitions of emotional intelligence share is that emotional intelligence is a personality trait.

It was the faddish decade of the 1990s that ushered in the craze for emotional intelligence tests. An editorial in the journal *Intelligence* in 1993 argued for the existence of an emotional intelligence trait; science journalist Daniel Goleman wrote a best-seller: *Emotional Intelligence*, with the instructive sub-title, *Why it can matter more than IQ*; and *Time* Magazine had a cover featuring 'EQ'. By 1997 there were several EQ scales and, inevitably, vigorous debate about their reliability and validity.

The fashion in management circles of speaking of one's ability to recognise the meanings of emotions and feelings as 'intelligence' can be viewed as either a trivial redefinition of cognitive intelligence, or yet another attempt by psychologists to impose a personality perspective on the community by asserting that emotional intelligence is a personality trait. That it is the latter perspective which has excited psychologists and seduced a gullible public is illustrated and supported by the number of 'emotional intelligence' (EQ) tests competing for managers' purses. A popular view is that EQ includes everything related to success (variously defined) that is not measured by IQ. Now while IQ does indeed predict job performance to a modest degree, there is no evidence that EQ (whatever it means) does so. This suggests that, unlike IQ – which is a measure of abilities – conceptualising and measuring EQ as a personality trait condemns it to suffer the same fate as the other personality traits. And like personality traits, there is no general agreement among psychologists about their meaning: extraversion means 'sociability' for American psychologists and 'changeability' for English psychologists. Cognitive intelligence has been reasonably defined; emotional intelligence has not. Definitions range from specific cognitive abilities to amorphous models that include personality and motivational traits; and there is considerable overlap in the measurement of cognitive and emotional intelligence. It is difficult to resist the conclusion that the popularity of emotional intelligence is faddish and little more than low-grade personality research. This is surely a disappointing conclusion after thirty years of attempts by psychologists to define and measure the construct. In short, the field is a mess and a mass of propaganda.

By the 1990s, emotional intelligence was firmly entrenched in management training courses and seriously promoted by human resource managers, especially females. If females saw emotional intelligence as an ability that they possessed to a greater degree than males, it is understandable that they would promote it. And promote it they did.

It is clear that emotional intelligence in the twenty-first century is not intended to mean what it meant to the ancient Greeks. Rather, the proponents of emotional intelligence inverted the views of the ancients by promoting the expression of feelings as a substitute for, or inversion of, rational thinking. And since some feminists associate rational thinking with some of the worst excesses of masculinity, it is easy to understand why emotional intelligence would appeal to them. As more females enter the ranks of management and seek competitive advantage, some will seek to invert the fundamental assumptions of the (male-dominated) Western rational tradition – which extols rational, critical thinking and indicts the expression of feelings. A feminist inversion of values, therefore, would involve the idea that expressing feelings should be valued and encouraged. Those individuals who retire behind the façade of rational thinking can be considered 'emotionally suppressed'. High EQ can then be interpreted as a positive virtue. Managers, especially males, who do not value the expression of personal feelings will need to be trained to overcome their inhibitions. In proportion as expressing one's feelings is encouraged, arguing with one's colleagues is discouraged. There is a logical reason for this. Propositions which express feelings are neither true nor false, whereas propositions which describe a state of affairs must be either true or false. Arguments are either valid or invalid, and feelings are, well, feelings.

There is an important relationship between the various functions of language and personal values. For example, managers who emphasise 'commanding' language betray a value system which differs from those who emphasise 'suggesting' language, which is why they are called the Ten Commandments and not the Ten Suggestions. Similarly, managers who argue value clarity of thinking because they realise that descriptive propositions are often ambiguous: metaphors abound and one has to make due allowance for them. When we say that a person's mind has gone blank we recognise the metaphor. But when we state that a person's mind is ill, we are less likely to do so. When it is claimed that managers are scientists, artists, politicians, coaches, captains or leaders, we are clearly in the grip of metaphor. As if this isn't enough, the management literature is replete with oxymorons (two words which yield a self-contradiction: military intelligence; entrepreneurial management; fun run); pleonasms (two words which yield a redundancy: strategic management; reverting back; freezing cold); and tautologies (expanded pleonasms: leaders influence people; charismatics have special personal qualities; managers are paid professionals).

Lynda Spillane found that managers in the Australian public service did not like to argue with their colleagues, preferring to employ the language of technical authority.[1] Her findings are consistent with local research which shows that managers favour a collaborative style of communication which shuns argument because of the fear that it might generate conflict. The desire to avoid overt conflict in work relationships, and the inability to cope with it when it arises, is a recurring theme in studies of Australian managers who describe the essential elements of the management relationship as trust, honesty, fairness and respect. The majority of the managers in her study acknowledged that they rarely argued with their colleagues because it involves excessive emotion and is rarely, if ever, constructive. Arguing, they thought, was a last resort when questioning failed. Managers saw arguing as stating one's point of view and putting forward negative sentiments for the opposite view, which is a pointless waste of time. Arguing was also seen as an invitation to engage in aggressive behaviour which reduces their authority. Thus, the widespread use of 'it seems to me', 'in my opinion', and 'subjectively speaking' as defences against criticism. This view of argument is far removed from the ancients Greeks and Ellis who valued argument as the sign of intellectual maturity.

To argue is to give reasons to support one's description of a state of affairs. And this is why the Western intellectual tradition, which has for more than 2500 years based itself squarely on argument as the vehicle for personal and social development, is called the Western rational tradition. Or at least it was until the arrival of postmodernists.

What, then, are we to make of the role of emotional intelligence in management? It has been said that IQ gets one hired and EQ gets one promoted. Such assertions are based on claims, by Daniel Goleman for example, that emotional intelligence predicts success in producing effective teamwork. However, he is unable to cite published empirical evidence to support his assertion. While there are many anecdotal, impressionistic and self-serving accounts, there are no empirical studies which show that emotional intelligence predicts management performance. Most of the popular claims about the relationship between emotional intelligence and work success are misleading and pretentious. They are misleading because they pretend to be offering empirical evidence, when they are in fact relying on impression and propaganda.

Once the idea of multiple intelligences is accepted there is no limit to the number of specific types which can be defined, discussed and measured – cognitive, emotional, social, political, organisational, leadership, business, money-making, criminal, alcoholic, musical, moral, spiritual, and so on. The old theory of multiple intelligences has never been more popular and there are many books, popular and academic, extolling the virtues of diverse types of intelligence. Indeed, one is drawn to the conclusion that there are as many types of human intelligence as there are types of human ability. Is the ability to make a cup of coffee an example of (coffee-making) intelligence? We have a right to wonder why authors insist on referring to specific abilities as intelligences, especially when many abilities are not correlated with measures of cognitive intelligence.

One of the appealing aspects of the theory of multiple intelligences is that it allows all people to be intelligent in their own way and thus maintain self-esteem. One may be deficient in mathematical intelligence, but espousing particular values – spiritual intelligence – can serve as a self-enhancing substitute. For example, if we have low emotional intelligence, we could be blessed with high spiritual intelligence.

A brochure advertising a workshop on Spiritual Intelligence stated that SQ is firmly grounded in quantum physics and neurophysiology. As quantum physics is a system of mechanics used to explain the behaviour of atoms, molecules and elementary particles, it is difficult to see how it could provide support for spiritual intelligence, whatever that term means. The brochure states that SQ is unique to human beings and is what we use to develop our capacity for vision, values, and purpose. Apparently, SQ enables us to inspire others and be inspired ourselves. Furthermore, it represents the 'power of inner leadership' which is truly miraculous given that 'leadership' is a relationship between leader and followers. Presumably, 'inner' leadership means that one part of us (the spiritual) leads and the other (the non-spiritual?) follows. The workshops were over-subscribed.

Once they leave the intellectual slums of spiritual intelligence, managers are confronted by books on 'moral' intelligence. An example is *Moral Intelligence* by Lennick and Kiel, with a recommendation from Daniel Goleman. Predictably, the book includes a 'measure' of moral intelligence – the Moral Competency Inventory (MCI). Morally intelligent individuals allegedly value integrity, responsibility, compassion and forgiveness. The authors make two claims. First, they believe that these (quintessentially Christian) values are to be praised and promoted. Second, they claim that managers need to espouse these values if they are to prosper. They assert that: there is a 'powerful' correlation between strong moral principles and business success, which may be true; and the moral principles which guarantee success are integrity, responsibility, compassion and forgiveness, which is not true.

A consequence of Lennick's and Kiel's view is that people with high moral intelligence reject and invert the values espoused by Niccolo Machiavelli and popularised by such television programs as *Yes Minister*. Machiavellians, therefore, have low moral intelligence since they do not support or promote notions of compassion, forgiveness or brotherly love. Lennick and Kiel support the Christian proverb 'honesty is the best policy', rather than the Machiavellian alternative 'those who tell the truth get their heads bashed in.' Interestingly, Machiavelli does not appear in Lennick's and Kiel's index.

In the 1960s psychologists caught up with the great Florentine author of *The Prince* who died in 1527. Psychologists plundered the book and, inevitably, constructed 'Machiavellian scales' which generated hundreds of research papers. Studies repeatedly showed that individuals who endorse Machiavelli's views about the importance of power, audacity, ruthlessness, cunning and deceit are emotionally detached, while those who are opposed to these values are sentimental and emotionally involved with others. Scores on Mach scales are unrelated to political affiliation, mental illness and cognitive intelligence and negatively related to emotional and moral intelligence. People with high Mach scores are aggressive, assertive risk-takers, manipulative, dogmatic, high achievers and masculine.

In short, Machiavellians are tough- minded individuals. There is some evidence that they perform better than tender-minded folk in bargaining relationships and are adept at discovering and exploiting personal weaknesses in others. Obviously, Machiavellians lie more and confess less than more sentimental people so that their answers to personality tests cannot be taken at face value. After all, Machiavellians do not admit that they are Machiavellian.

Opinion is still divided about Machiavelli. Clearly he was an anti-Christian writer. But he was also a man of great intelligence who wrote about the realities of politics. If he lacked moral intelligence it is because he understood the political necessity of 'entering into evil when necessity commands'.

The moral intelligence movement in management represents the tender-minded alternative to Machiavellianism. By emphasising the importance of integrity, responsibility, compassion and forgiveness, it sets itself against the pagan values of power. If the meek and the mild are to inherit the earth, Christian values of love, compassion and forgiveness must predominate, otherwise the meek and the mild shall be fodder for Machiavelli's ruthless pagans. The moral intelligence movement, therefore, seeks to continue the Christian fight against paganism in management. And their crusaders use the social sciences to help them in their fight.

Managers all do a little harmless moralising from time to time simply because they cannot avoid value judgements when they make decisions. However, there are some who believe that they know, in a very strong sense of the term 'know', precisely how people should act or be prevented from acting, and such is their faith in their own ability to discern how every type of activity will affect the destiny of humanity that they love to infect others with their version of right belief. This is not intelligence, it is moralism, and in my experience many psychologists, trainers and consultants suffer from it in a most virulent form.

In management studies no one has discovered how to do anything new, or for that matter worked out what sort of thing they ought to discover. This leaves an open field for moralists. One author promotes Christian values and another endorses the prescriptions of Machiavelli. In other words, they are frequently animated by personal value judgements and ever ready to point us towards the path of greater righteousness.

To define a management problem as a moral problem is to imply that managers could eliminate it by choosing to do so; and this implies that they already know how to do so and that the remedy is within their power. If this were true, managers would have no need of trying to develop a social science: they could already solve all the problems that worry moralists. If one believes that management problems can be eliminated by persuading people to make the requisite moral choices then one should remove oneself from management and join a seminary.

The management training situation is quite plain. When HR managers, psychologists and trainers allow themselves to become evangelists for social reform they betray their vocation. Their example is soon followed by their colleagues who take to talking of events in terms of whether they should or should not be allowed to happen regardless of whether such control is within our powers. The problem of distinguishing between what changes it is within our power to make, and what states of affairs are determined by factors beyond our present control, simply disappears because it is assumed that nothing social is beyond our control. History and current affairs both mock this attitude but it proves difficult to counter and it exposes the weaknesses in management education and training and indeed in all the social sciences: the inability to come to grips with any way of identifying precisely what is determined by forces other than human choice.

7

THE RSI DEBACLE

Pain: Absence of pleasure. Maximised in blue-collar workers; minimised in management.

In Australia in the 1980s large numbers of working people complained of pain, generally in the wrist. They were told that they were suffering from Repetition Strain Injury (RSI), later to be renamed Retrospective Supplementary Income by those of a more cynical bent. RSI was an example of the progressive medicalisation of work behaviour in which notions of 'illness', 'treatment' and 'patient' figure prominently. The RSI phenomenon – or debacle – can be used as a case study of the tendency in Australian occupational health circles to emphasise medical rather than moral behaviour at work. This tendency, stimulated by professional interests, has retarded work reform strategies which aimed to increase autonomy for all working people.

One of the goals which guided work reform strategies in the Western democracies since the 1970s was autonomy for all workers. Scandinavian experiments with semi-autonomous work groups and the redesign of offices and factories were widely viewed as important steps in this direction. While work reform strategies in Australia were much discussed in the 1970s – especially job enrichment programs and industrial democracy – Australian work environments showed little evidence of progress in these directions. Furthermore, managers and trade unionists tended to psychologise employment relations, exemplified by the myth of 'the careless worker' who caused unnecessary accidents, and the myth of the 'chronically dissatisfied worker' who caused unnecessary tension. The habit of looking to the personality of employees rather than factors in the work environment as explanations of work problems was especially characteristic of Australian managers in the 1980s and remains so to this day. The popularity of personality tests and training courses which focus on personality, motivation and now, emotional intelligence, illustrates and supports this contention.

As we have seen, Australian managers have long embraced the idea that performance has to be weighed against personality factors if working people are to 'get on with each other'. A consequence of managers concerning themselves with the personalities of their colleagues is that, sooner or later, they will be forced to deal with psychological as well as practical problems. If psychological problems are related to work activities managers do not need to involve themselves in the internal workings of their colleagues' psyches. However, this is not the path Australian managers chose to follow. On the contrary, they actively turned their attention away from the work environment (which was the primary concern of trade union officials) toward the inner life of their colleagues. Involving themselves in psychological matters may not have been a sound move for managers but it was a godsend for management consultants, especially psychologists. Theories of motivation, personality, leadership, communication and team-building, proliferated while concurrently managers were required to undertake personality and intelligence tests to determine person-organisation 'fit'.

Relations between working people, like all human relations, are fraught with difficulties, especially where they are based explicitly on power relationships. Understandably, Australian managers work hard to minimise the effects of the overt application of power by a variety of means, including the myth that the workplace is a home away from home where work relations are treated as quasi-family relations. This has the obvious consequence that managers are quasi-parents and their subordinates are quasi-children. If accepted, this paternalistic strategy euphemises workplace language and disguises the reality of managerial power. Since one form of paternalism leads easily to other forms, it is inevitable that managers/parents become embroiled in the illnesses of their subordinates/children.

Clearly, subordinates in power relationships express their discontents in more covert ways than do managers. Thus, subordinates often use metaphors and symbolism to communicate their dissatisfaction. In Christian societies, one way to express discontent symbolically is to claim that one is unwell, in pain or ill. Responses to such claims are not supposed to be hostile or indifferent so that people who adopt the role of sick patient are considered to be acting honestly and ethically. In short, complaining of feeling unwell is a gesture calling forth a positive response from another person. This is what qualifies the relationship as moral since issues of right and wrong behaviour are involved, especially on the part of the person who responds to the 'sufferer'. The last word has to be put in quotes because it is possible that a person who complains is not in fact unwell, but is seeking support, attention, affection, love or some other reward. The point is that since we cannot experience the state of well-being of others, we infer it from their behaviour and words. A complaint about a sore neck might be a legitimate expression of a pain in the neck or it might be a lie, giving another meaning to 'pain in the neck'.

If moral conflicts are treated on their merits, issues of right and wrong are worked through, if not to resolution, at least to an understanding of the underlying problems involved. It is a cliché that complaints about a leaking tap are often symbolic expressions of more serious complaints (about money, supervisors, etc.): they are symbolic expressions by people in subordinate positions because overt complaints may result in unacceptable retaliation from those with more power.

However, if moral conflicts are redefined so as to invalidate issues of right and wrong, those who complain of problems are likewise invalidated. One effective way to disarm critics is to declare them mentally ill and thus invalidate their complaints: Stalin dispatched large numbers of Soviet dissidents to the Gulag, labelling them as 'soft schizophrenics'. Similarly, when American slaves escaped from their chains, they were not treated as human beings who had moral grievances, but as organisms who were suffering from an illness called drapetomania, a 'medical condition' invented in the U.S. in the nineteenth century and applied only to slaves who attempted to escape to freedom.

One way to deprive people of autonomy is to treat their moral conflicts as medical conditions for which they are not responsible and which require medical treatment. Policies and practices which treat moral dilemmas (behaviourally manifested) as if they are illnesses (physically manifested) create a therapeutic paternalism where people are 'demoralised', that is, they are regarded as medical patients rather than moral agents.

In Australia, legal cases have involved the 'demoralising' and medicalising of conflicts at work. In *Anderson Meat Packing Company v. Giacomantonio*, a worker was judged to be incapacitated for work while 'demoralised' after 'seeing' God in the cool-room of the meat-works.[1] The use of the word 'demoralised' is surely significant because it suggests that people who report distress at work may lose their capacity for rational, and thus moral, behaviour and so cannot be considered responsible agents. In this way a moral issue – a man wanted to get out of the cool-room – is medicalised.

Pain and discomfort have long been recognised as occupational hazards. For decades medical practitioners have noted the prevalence of simple muscle complaints among process workers. Medical intervention was rarely required and the problems were usually overcome by rest and prevented by uncomplicated changes to work practices and appropriate training. In a small minority of cases the problems were diagnosed as tenosynovitis, which had been associated with work activity and relieved by conservative medical treatment.

Researchers advised all parties to consider the influence of psychosocial factors both in and beyond the workplace because these were important in the incidence, persistence and prevention of such complaints.

In 1976 an industrial health group at the Liverpool Women's Health Centre in Sydney, published a booklet called *Your Job: His Profit or Your Life*, which provided information on tenosynovitis. The following year a Workers' Health Centre was established at Lidcombe (NSW) and a Workers' Health Action Group in Melbourne. These centres were influential in drawing attention to 'repetitive injuries' as a serious occupational health issue since more than half the workers treated at workers' health centres suffered from what was later called Repetition Strain Injury (RSI). In an article entitled 'A Crippling New Epidemic in Industry', published in *New Doctor* in 1979, these 'injuries' were attributed to the inadequacies of the medical profession and legal/compensation policies and practices.

Prior to the late 1970s RSI was unknown in occupational medicine. Government compensation statistics showed that the number of musculoskeletal disorders had been relatively static for many years. Statistically, the RSI 'epidemic' commenced around 1979 and continued well into the 1980s when it sharply declined. The increases could not be explained by changes in the size or composition of the workforce, the nature of work processes, or the way official statistics were compiled. In NSW, for example, the number of musculoskeletal cases increased from 670 (1976–1977) to 4550 (1983–1984), an unparalleled increase. By 1983–1984 RSI represented 28.5%

of total cases in NSW compensation statistics. Females accounted for about 65% of claims which partly reflects the proportion of females in jobs that involve repetitive tasks. It remains to be tested whether females engaged in repetitive tasks are more likely than males to act like patients.

Large organisations, particularly in the public sector, recorded similar increases. Unofficial estimates placed the national total in excess of 20,000 and almost 4000 cases were recorded in Australian Government organisations in the December 1985 quarter alone. The incidence pattern was, however, inconsistent with exposure to repetitive tasks. Some organisations remained unaffected, whereas others, including Telecom, with similar work patterns, reported outbreaks of 'epidemic' proportions. Of those organisations massively affected, some revealed a pattern which suggested a contagion effect in that workers were affected in quick succession.

Clearly, Australians in the 1980s were involved in an epidemic – of compensation claims. But what were people seeking claims for? Did the extraordinarily rapid rise in claims correspond to an underlying incidence of musculoskeletal injuries? Or was the epidemic one of mass hysteria? Or was it mass malingering?

Historically and unsurprisingly, workers' compensation cases recorded under the classification 'Synovitis, Bursitis, Tenosynovitis' generally affected blue-collar, factory workers. But by the early 1980s a new incidence pattern emerged. No longer were these injuries exclusively associated with semi-skilled workers on production lines. Keyboard operators and clerical workers in traditionally 'safe' white-collar jobs began reporting these injuries in increasingly large numbers. As claims for compensation mounted and test cases were decided in favour of the complainants, insurance premiums skyrocketed.

In the early 1980s, researchers at the Australian Council of Trade Unions (ACTU) were collecting data on tenosynovitis, cervico-brachial injury and what the Workers' Health Centre in NSW called 'repetitive movement injuries'. The ACTU issued guidelines in August 1982 in which the major author, John Mathews, coined the term 'repetitive strain injury' to widen the scope from 'movement' to 'strain' incurred at, say, a poorly designed keyboard. Mathews was influenced in his thinking by white-collar jobs with new computer-based word-processing systems in the Australian Taxation Office, where word- processing targets of 12,000 keystrokes per hour, without rest breaks, were common. The purpose of the ACTU recommendations was to encourage unions to negotiate limits on repetitive activity and regular breaks. The unions were spectacularly successful in having these demands met. The front line in this endeavour was to be the unions' elected safety representatives. It was Mathews' intention to have Australian workplaces peopled by worker representatives who would monitor conditions and ensure that employers were meeting their 'duty of care'. The ACTU guidelines were conceived, therefore, as guides for these workplace negotiations. Importantly, Mathews' document was critical of those who want to screen individuals medically to determine susceptibility to RSI. He noted that treating RSI medically yielded depressingly poor results.[2]

National concern about RSI and its costs to the community resulted in the Australian Government establishing two independent enquiries which recommended substantial changes to the design of work. Whereas earlier approaches to the prevention of RSI concentrated on biomechanical factors – posture, speed, etc. – the RSI Committee report observed that this approach was relatively ineffective since some organisations had spent large sums of money on work-stations only to find that the problem remained.

By 1986 RSI was known as 'Retrospective Supplementary Income', 'Runaway Social Invention', 'Golden Wrist', and 'Kangaroo Paw'. It was listed in the 'International Classification of Diseases' of the World Health Organisation among the Somatoform disorders, which is a subset of mental and behavioural disorders, including writer's cramp, occupational neurosis and conversion hysteria.

The RSI debate became acrimonious and speakers at public forums were frequently abused and threatened, as I can attest from personal experience. Critics of the orthodox medical interpretation were accused of supporting insurance companies and of gross insensitivity to the suffering of their fellow citizens. Out of this often ill-tempered debate four perspectives emerged, although only three were widely discussed in public forums and professional articles.

The medical perspective dominated the debate and the government commissions. RSI was assumed to be a medical condition which can be diagnosed and treated. The injury is attributed to biomechanical factors, such as inadequate work practices, which must be rectified to prevent further injury.

Injured workers are treated conservatively (rest) or actively (physiotherapy, surgery). This perspective was endorsed by the National Occupational Health and Safety Commission, but it slighted the influence of psychosocial factors and gave RSI a medical legitimacy that was unwarranted because of the absence, in the vast majority of cases, of the necessary clinical signs which are needed for a valid diagnosis. The medical view was that RSI is a physical condition of traumatic origin caused by biomechanical factors. It was widely promoted by medical practitioners even though they were not able validly to explain RSI's epidemiology or its distribution in the workplace.

The official opposition within the medical profession came from psychiatry. RSI is not a physical condition but a psychiatric one, probably conversion hysteria. Some psychiatric conditions closely mimic physical illness and have been known to occur en masse in industrial settings. Various psychological problems at home and at work cause psychological conflict which manifests in this symbolic disorder. Consequently, complainants require psychotherapy to resolve their personal problems. This perspective was promoted by several psychiatrists, orthopaedic surgeons and rheumatologists, some of whom were employed by insurance companies to give evidence in legal proceedings. If RSI is a neurosis which is not occupational in origin, it is not compensable.

A third view was that RSI is neither a medical nor a psychiatric condition, but malingering. Most complainants are faking pain and cheating society. RSI is, therefore, a hoax consciously used (though not invented) by workers to gain rewards. This perspective caused a public furore because it simultaneously impugned the motives of workers and the diagnostic skills of the medical profession. It was widely discussed in the media and defended by anonymous authors.

Leigh Deves and I defended a fourth perspective.[3] RSI can be characterised as a social movement based on a system of rewards applied to people who complain of pain (and other discomforts – tingling, weakness) at work. Consequently, people who are essentially healthy but experience pain choose to complain about pain rather than adopt a stoical attitude thereto. Defenders of this perspective were labelled 'social constructionists' and dismissed because it was claimed that they, or their arguments, supported insurance companies in their efforts to blame the victims and avoid paying workers' compensation. They did not.

While these four perspectives cannot be reconciled because they differ on fundamental assumptions about the causes and nature of RSI, the one theme which links them is that of pain and the reporting of pain. The reporting of pain is intimately bound up with the role of 'patient', just as the treatment of pain is bound up with the role of doctor. One may adopt the patient role with or without pain, just as one may treat a person who has or does not have pain.

The accepted medical criterion for diagnosing illness is the presence of a physical sign, (i.e. a demonstrable physicochemical alteration of the body), with or without symptoms (e.g. experiences of pain). The notion of RSI derives its main support from known medical conditions, such as tenosynovitis or carpal tunnel syndrome, with which it is erroneously equated. A condition like tenosynovitis is diagnosed by its signs (inflammation) and symptoms (pain). In the majority of cases of RSI, however, (perhaps as many as 90% according to some researchers), diagnosis is made on symptoms alone: on the basis of a communication or complaint.

The idea of RSI is thus firmly based on complaining, unlike established diseases which are based on independent medical signs. Symptoms without signs are communications not diseases, complaints not 'conditions', until proven otherwise. The fact that medical diagnoses are made on the basis of symptoms alone does not mean they are valid, or responsible.

Critics challenged this argument claiming that:

> Spillane and Deves support this position by arguing that where symptoms exist, without physical signs, they should not be treated as diseases but rather as complaints or communications. This argument is based largely on uncritical acceptance of the familiar claim that where medical practitioners are unable to identify physical signs of injury it cannot be presumed to exist...It is also possible that medical practitioners really lack the diagnostic skills or the technology to identify the signs. Spillane and Deves overlook this possibility and, after noting claims, (disputed elsewhere), that up to 90% of diagnoses of RSI rely on reports of subjective symptoms, they conclude that the assumption that RSI pain arises from repetitive movement at work 'is unwarranted on the evidence.[4]

Never was a challenge so easily met. The critics were clearly confused about diseases and their diagnosis. In the

Western medical tradition the fundamental axiom is that valid diagnoses of disease are based on *signs*. Historically, if people who complained of pain or discomfort in the wrist were found to have physical signs – say inflammation – they were probably diagnosed with tenosynovitis. In the case of RSI, the majority of diagnoses were based on symptoms alone since there were no signs. It is of course true that medical practitioners often base their putative diagnoses on symptoms alone. In the absence of signs, however, diagnosticians can at best suggest possibilities. They may be right or they may be wrong. But they cannot maintain the position that medicine is objective and scientific while basing their diagnoses on subjective criteria: their impressions or inferences. Putative diagnoses are not real diagnoses and putative illnesses are not real illnesses. While the public is frequently told what medical practitioners and experts 'believe' or 'assume' to be the facts about conditions like RSI (or ADHD, depression, schizophrenia, bipolar disorder and a host of other 'conditions' diagnosed on the basis of symptoms alone), their beliefs or assumptions are not facts. In law people are presumed innocent until proven guilty; in medicine people are assumed healthy until proven ill. That doctors or their apologists diagnose medical and psychiatric illnesses without evidence is an example of 'medical mugging'.

RSI was based on complaints of pain (or discomfort). Clearly, one person cannot experience another person's pain. Pain cannot be observed directly, although it is often inferred from a person's communications: the experience of pain is private and the expression of pain is public. When people say they have pain we may believe them because they appear to be distressed, or we may choose to believe that they are pretending to have pain for some unstated reason. The point is that we can only guess. We may seek reasons to support our belief: their history of physical illness, their tendency to complain or act stoically, the logic and politics of the situation they find themselves in, and so on. Furthermore, our own value system may tend to predispose us to believe they are ill or malingering. Logically, then, since pain and discomfort are subjective experiences, unlike, say, epileptic convulsions, the actual incidence of malingering in conditions like RSI (and mental illnesses generally) can never be known.

When people experience pain they can communicate it, complain about it, or conceal it. Those who complain of pain may go on to define themselves as patients. A person can experience pain but choose not to be a patient. Or a person can choose to be a patient without the experience of pain. Since people generally act as they are rewarded, and if complaining of pain is rewarded, some (and in the case of RSI, many) people will choose to become patients (with or without pain).

Alternatively, some people who are treated by doctors and psychiatrists as patients do not suffer from an illness and do not want to be patients. When people with pain are told that they may be in the first stage of a crippling disease which demands urgent medical treatment, both illness and patient role are applied to the experience of pain. Furthermore, turning people into patients exposes them to a medical/ legal game which few understand or escape from happily. If they are not labelled as sick patients they risk being labelled as mentally ill or malingerers. It was difficult in the 1980s to adopt a humane approach to this problem when workers claimed managers made them ill and managers retaliated with company doctors, psychiatrists, lawyers and accusations of malingering.

Pain is an inexorable aspect of the human condition and the causes of much chronic discomfort remain a mystery. When people suggest possible causes of their discomfort the responses they encounter from family, friends and doctors influence their subsequent behaviour. When working people with pain complain about their working conditions and their views are ignored or criticised, some choose to communicate their dissatisfaction by becoming patients. Where the work climate encourages medicalising work behaviour or rewarding illness, some people are easily induced to become patients. Thus morals are confused with medicine, values with Valium.

RSI was a social movement and not a medical epidemic. It was characterised by a significant increase in the number of people who, in the absence of diagnosable signs, chose to become, or were defined by others, as patients. Logically, though not empirically, it can be asserted that some experienced pain and others did not. While this logical conclusion is obvious, many people during the RSI era became angry at the very thought that anyone would suggest that some workers are malingerers. On the other side, some people took the unwarranted position that all, or the majority of RSI complainants were cheats and malingerers. Sadly, logical reasoning was not a feature of the RSI debate.

Before the invention of RSI, workers experiencing pain were neither encouraged nor inclined to adopt the helpless and dependent role of patient. And neither did they seek to use their discomfort politically, despite the availability of this line of redress, either because their problems were dealt with locally or they risked penalties for complaining. When, at the height of the RSI 'epidemic', Deves and I visited the U.S. to enquire about similar experiences, the general response was that if workers complained of work-related pain they would be penalised. This left open the possibility that repetitive work was causing widespread problems which, for obvious reasons, went unreported. In American workplaces there were no incentives and severe penalties for becoming patients with pain. Rather than support the medical or psychiatric perspectives, however, this fact supports the conclusion that RSI was a social movement built on the attitudes to work and health adopted by the Australian community, especially its occupational health, legal and compensation arms. In Skinnerian language, complaining of pain was positively reinforced.

In the 1980s, the historical pattern changed from cooperation to confrontation. Warring parties sought the advice of medical and legal experts to justify an adversarial position. In the absence of clinical signs of physical illness, workers were accused of malingering or treated as mentally ill. Having had their motives impugned and personal experiences invalidated, workers retaliated through medical certification and many were removed from work for indefinite periods. Medical certification guaranteed them access to a compensation system which did not encourage recovery. Personal activity was discouraged because insurance companies employed private investigators whose evidence, admissible in industrial courts, could prove embarrassing to plaintiffs. Faced with the prospect of jeopardising their claims many workers adopted, or were placed in, a state of dependency leading to iatrogenic consequences, such as anxiety and depression. These secondary conditions led to further medical treatment or psychotherapy. Dependency was thus required and promoted through medical and legal intervention, which probably accounts for the persistence of symptoms beyond reasonable expectations.

RSI is not and never has been medically recognised for clinical purposes. The term is a residue constructed from differential diagnostic practice. According to the inventor of the term, my Macquarie University colleague John Mathews, it was never intended for use in legal proceedings. The ACTU's 1982 recommendations crossed an invisible line; the prevention of RSI was different from the prevention of occupational deafness where the physical cause was clear. How one felt became an issue for the courts.

That RSI gained widespread acceptance in medical and legal proceedings is the result of injudicious medical practices: RSI was consistently referred to as 'a crippling disease of epidemic proportions'. Managers' clumsy efforts to substitute malingering or mental illness served only to stiffen trade unionists' resolve to fight this 'illness' medically. Government reports compounded the problem by issuing codes of practice that failed to take account of psychological factors, even though researchers had emphasised their importance. For example, one of my studies showed that satisfaction with one's supervisor and control over one's work were better predictors of RSI complaints than were biomechanical factors.[5] Worse still, the guidelines provided by the National Occupational Health and Safety Commission, though ostensibly aimed at constructive work reform, resulted in establishing coercive work routines, standardising work, and scrutinising workers. These guidelines were almost the exact opposite of the work reform strategies and practices which emerged from occupational research during the 1970s which sought to maximise autonomy for all working people.

The legally sanctioned use of the medical model in Australian workplaces has led to the increased power of medical practitioners and psychiatrists to determine who is healthy and who is ill, and the increased dependency of those who adopt, or are allocated to, the role of patient. Given the predilection of doctors to diagnose conditions in the absence of clinical signs and to transform moral dilemmas into medical conditions, it is difficult to see an end to therapeutic paternalism.

The RSI 'epidemic', which represented a ten-fold increase in claims for compensation, has subsided. In the late 1980s trade unions modified their prevention campaigns while the Australian Medical Association and the Royal Australian College of Physicians criticised the concept of RSI and called for a new name. They got it. Unbelievably, RSI is now known as Occupational Overuse Syndrome, which indicates that we have learned little from the 1980s. Bruce Hocking, one-time

Medical Director at Telecom, provided convincing evidence that there was no relationship between RSI and technology or the ergonomics of the work station. His research revealed that 83% of complainants were female with younger age groups and part-time workers over-represented in the statistics. Among typists and computer operators, the fastest and busiest reported the *lowest* proportion of cases, a similar finding to that of the Departmental Committee into Telegraphists' Cramp in 1911.[6] A much publicised legal case, *Cooper versus Commonwealth of Australia* (1987), was lost. Finally, the *Medical Journal of Australia* closed correspondence on RSI between 1988 and 1991, and then reactivated it in 1993.

In 1995 a consensus statement, published by the Australian Faculty of Occupational Medicine, attributed the causes of the RSI 'epidemic' to: technological change; poor management practices (failure to address workers' complaints); unions' increased attention to workers' health and safety (and compensation for work-related illness); the spread of RSI from blue-collar to white-collar workers and publicity about large compensation payouts (some of which were sensationalist and irresponsible); workers' discontent transformed into 'illness'; medical practitioners' confusion about diagnosis, pathogenesis, treatment and prognosis; RSI support groups that reinforced patienthood; and government reports that enshrined a mechanistic model of RSI instead of considering psychological factors.[7]

After the promulgation of the Workers' Compensation Act in 1987 large lump-sum payments through common law claims dropped dramatically in NSW. Claims for 'Occupational

Overuse Syndrome' halved in the period 1995–6 and 1999–2000 and claims accepted decreased from 1333 to 179.

The medicalisation of work behaviour continues, however. In the 1990s RSI gave way to an even bigger 'epidemic': occupational stress. Combining an insensitivity to language with an ignorance of the lessons learned from the RSI debacle, government authorities now refer to occupational stress as 'psychological injury' which, because of the word 'injury', ensures that it became a matter of legal disputation.

Stress costs more than $1.3 billion per year in Australia and stress claims are increasing while other claims are decreasing. Between 1996–1997 and 2003–2004, claims for all injuries and illnesses decreased by 13% while stress claims during that period increased by 83%. In 2002–2004 claims for 'psychological injury' accounted for 7% of total workers' compensation claims but nearly 27% of total costs of claims. Sydney psychiatrist Yolande Lucire has it right when she argued in *Constructing* RSI that when the occupational stress epidemic replaced the RSI epidemic in the early 1990s, the medical profession was poised to medicalise as psychological injury the consequences of abrasive and dysfunctional relationships, overwork and understaffing.

Since many stress claims are based on moral problems, such as getting on with people at work, we need to rethink the issue of what constitutes an 'injury' and 'illness' and allow the possibility that we misuse these concepts at our peril. This is especially the case with 'psychological injury' which, as a substitute for 'stress', raises more problems than it solves.

8

STRESS AND CONTROLLABILITY

Stress: Overstressed feature of management life, but only in the sense that managers impose it on others; quasi-medical condition used to avoid work. 'Stressed' is 'desserts' spelt backwards.

Nietzsche believed that individuals who calculate the value of each day according to their degree of happiness are mere pawns in the game of life. Freedom, for Nietzsche, meant becoming more indifferent to stress and hard work. He promoted a philosophy based on energy, vitality and joyful striving and had little time for those who complain of the stresses of life. Nietzsche's tone – a product of the 1880s – is very different from the strident culture of complaint which characterises Western society today. Complaining about the stress of life has become so acceptably widespread that it takes a brave individual to adopt Nietzsche's philosophy and promote it openly.

Fifty years later, Sigmund Freud argued that modern society is characterised by 'civilised nervousness' and its dominant expression is the complaint about the difficulties of living in the modern era. The popularity of psychoanalysis in the twentieth century is testimony to the ubiquitous nature of complaining and the determination to institutionalise it. Institutionalising complaining has been combined with obsessing about personal rights. Taken together and ignoring personal responsibilities, a social movement built on stress has evolved which has assumed 'epidemic' proportions. Stress is no longer regarded as an important and inexorable part of life, and thus something to be valued. Rather, stress is nowadays regarded as a 'condition' to be treated, a 'symptom' of malaise, an infringement of one's rights, an assault upon one's psyche, a reason to engage in litigation, an example of coercion and harassment, a product of power politics, and an excuse for early retirement. Coupled with the assertion that we live in a rapidly changing world in which technology has overpowered sensitive people, the stress movement has grown to uncontainable dimensions.

'Stress' is borrowed from engineering and many of those who foist the concept on the public claim the prestige of science in justification. When the stress on bridges is too great they collapse. So by analogy, when the stress on individuals is too great they collapse. A philosophy of mechanics is thereby introduced into psychology and from there to the workplace and law courts. Individuals are transformed into machines which respond positively or negatively to forces brought to bear upon them. Individuals are, therefore, defenceless in the face of external pressures which invade them, so to speak. Resistance is ultimately futile since individuals cannot be held responsible for their behaviour because they are, strictly speaking, not individuals at all. They have few or no choices when faced with external pressures and after a certain point has been reached, collapse under their power. Where choice is not possible, responsibility is not relevant. This minefield of confusions and contradictions has captured the public imagination to such a degree that anyone who claims that stress is good is regarded as not quite sane.

Clearly, not all stress is negative and harmful to personal health and well-being: the only place one finds people without stress is a cemetery. Without the energy or stress which derives from stimulation, humans would lack the ability to solve practical problems and function effectively. Yet stress is widely regarded as a necessary evil. How did a universal human condition get such a bad reputation? Why do some people complain of stress while others thrive on it?

Before attempting to answer these questions it should be emphasised that there is no independent entity called 'stress' even though people talk and write about it as if it were a concrete noun. Stress is not, for example, a definable environmental noxious agent: indeed it is not objectively definable at all. Stress is a relational term: a metaphor employed to describe particular interactions between individuals and their environments. For example, people who lack or lose control over important aspects of their environment are likely to describe their situation as stressful.

Working with a difficult manager may lead to changes in bodily functioning (increased heart rate and hormonal secretions) and changes in feelings (tension and frustration). It is important to emphasise, however, that stressors cannot be abstracted from the individual's perception of them. This explains why a stressor produces an effort reaction for one person and distress for another. For example, researchers have found it difficult to demonstrate the harmful effects of noise because of the meaning attached to it; what is a source of musical pleasure for some is painful noise for others.

When interviewed about stress some people call on their powers of adaptability and endurance to deny that stress is important; they take the stand that one simply has to put up with stress for the sake of progress. Some are explicit about the view that those who complain about stress are neurotic, weak, unduly querulous or lacking in hardihood. Their attitude implies that they find some cause for pride in adapting: stress is something to be endured.

Some years ago I was a member of a research team of psychologists whose task was to investigate attitudes to aircraft noise. The team interviewed residents who lived directly under the aircraft flight path at Sydney airport. We wanted to know what the residents thought of living in an environment that was dominated by considerable, intermittent aircraft noise. Our first finding was that residents who lived further away from the flight path were more likely to refuse to be interviewed: they could see no reason to participate in the study since noise wasn't a problem for them. We therefore expected to hear more complaints about aircraft noise when we talked with residents closer to the flight path. Surprisingly, many residents under the flight path took the position that they simply had to put up with aircraft noise. Initially, we thought that this view was likely to be confined to those who worked with or around aircraft, but although this view was widely endorsed by such people, it was held by residents generally. Even though most of the residents admitted that aircraft noise was a nuisance, they took the view that it was something which could (and should) be endured. It did not press on them as immediately as their financial struggles. It was best ignored. Nevertheless, the research team believed there was something false about claims of imperturbability. The taped interviews contained cases where the effects of passing aircraft on conversation are plainly evident yet the residents said it bothered them not at all. This is the other side of the stress movement in which stoical responses disguise objective problems in living. For if most of the residents who were interviewed say they are not troubled by aircraft noise, and if these data are taken at their face value, they could be used to justify significant increases in air traffic or the building of airports near domestic residences.

Where individuals adopt the policy of calling on their powers of adaptation in this way, they become unreliable instruments for measuring the fitness of the environment, particularly for others who are not so inured. It is exactly this psychological phenomenon which has permitted the progressive process which is described as destruction of the environment. Excessive reliance on interviews and attitude surveys carries the risk of pointing us toward environments which approach the limits of human tolerance rather than towards better conditions.

The individualistic nature of the stress response has also created problems for researchers who rely on attitude surveys which invite a variety of strategic responses. This is especially true of surveys which use questions that are general, impersonal and do not raise the need for specific action. Such questions invite uncritical replies. For example, the following questions produce highly positive responses:

- Do you believe that you are doing something useful?
- Are you able to talk freely with your boss?
- Do you feel accepted by people in your group?

Questions which produce less conservative responses are those which emphasise 'anticipation', of being deliberately prepared for future changes:

- Is the person affected by a change of job sometimes the last one to know about it?
- Do your managers need training in human relations?
- Do you think that managers are good at explaining the reasons for their actions?

These questions involve particular themes: clarification of organisational goals; information about on-going activities; and education and personal development. When people are asked whether they are satisfied with their lives, their responses are generally positive: a mixture of resignation and accommodation. When people are asked questions about the future, and what is needed to understand and anticipate it, responses will be less positive. Perhaps a concern for the future creates anxiety, or the thought of a future much like the present creates apprehension. It is one thing to resign oneself to the present but quite another to see this as the norm for the future.

Several researchers have sought an explanation for how some people live with high levels of stress but do not fall victim to premature illness. They insist on the importance of 'stress buffers', behaviour patterns which allegedly protect people who experience considerable stress from consequent illness. The idea is that some people cope with stress because they do not behave stressfully when many people do. There follows the circular conclusion that they do not react stressfully because they are resistant to stress. These people are called hardy. Now if stress exists as an independent entity, no one could escape it and coping would have to be employed to minimise its effects. If, on the other hand, stress does not exist as such, then some people will refuse to admit that they are stressed.

Stress is a relationship between individuals and their environments and it cannot be understood apart from that relationship. It is well known, for example, that personal performance is related to levels of environmental stimulation. The Yerkes-Dodson Law states that the relationship between performance and level of stimulation can be expressed graphically as an inverted U, which means that performance is maximised at a moderate level of stimulation. Since humans need adequate levels of stimulation to function effectively, too little stimulation is accompanied by feelings of boredom, apathy, inactivity and low levels of performance. This can be as unhealthy as excessive stimulation, as shown by the rapid deterioration of many people after retirement. At the other extreme, too much stimulation is accompanied by irritability and anger so that performance deteriorates and can, in extreme cases, lead to illness. While some people appear to thrive on excessive stimulation there is a point beyond which performance deteriorates and health is affected adversely.

If individuals need to have a moderately varied flow of experiences, it follows that they also need to have a degree of control over their levels of stimulation. For example, people working in jobs which allow them to adjust levels of stimulation when they fall outside an acceptable range are less likely to report stress symptoms than those whose level of stimulation is beyond their control. Stress is not merely a problem of underload or overload: personal control must be taken into account.

Robert Karasek has pointed to the many contradictory findings in occupational stress research which can be traced to incomplete models derived from mutually exclusive research traditions.[1] One tradition emphasises job control and another job demands. Both traditions have to be analysed to avoid inconsistencies, such as the finding that both managers and assembly-line workers have stressful jobs, but the latter report higher levels of stress. One factor which might account for this difference is job control: the ability to moderate levels of demand. Karasek's studies of Swedish and American workers confirmed his prediction that people working in high demand and low control jobs would report the highest frequency of stress symptoms. Decreasing job demands alone is not an effective solution, however, since it leads to passivity and boredom. Workers in passive jobs reported the highest degree of non-participation in active leisure, demonstrating a 'carryover' from work to leisure and little evidence that deficiencies in the work environment are compensated for by choice of leisure activity. This finding has led some people to conclude that workers in passive jobs are a self-selected sample in that those with passive personalities are more likely to accept such jobs and remain in them. There is no convincing evidence to support this view, although it is widely entertained in management circles.

The lowest levels of stress symptoms and the highest levels of participation in social activity are found in people who work in jobs which offer high levels of control. Employees in low- discretion jobs, with little opportunity to use creative talents, report feelings of monotony, boredom and stress. These are more widespread and intense among employees who are young, well-educated and whose jobs are severely circumscribed as to variety, skill and social interaction.

The 1980s represented the halcyon days of occupational stress research in Australia. Rejecting questionnaire studies as crude and misleading, researchers used hormonal analysis to index the 'physiological cost' of work. Their research strategy was based on the following assumptions: there is a physiological cost attached to all jobs – in some cases the cost is high, in others low; this cost varies with the type of job and with individuals; this cost can be assessed independently of attitude or personality surveys by analysing 'stress' hormones – adrenaline, noradrenaline and cortisol. Numerous studies have shown that reports of anxiety and aggression are correlated with elevated levels of adrenaline and noradrenaline respectively. Feelings of depression, hopelessness and helplessness are related to elevated levels of cortisol and suppression of the immune response, suggesting possible relationships with particular illnesses. While it is not possible to say that a certain level of hormonal secretion is an indicator of distress that is harmful to the health of an individual, there is considerable evidence of an association between chronically elevated cortisol levels and the incidence of degenerative disease.

In an elegant study, Jack Bassett established that there are two stages in the stress-induced development of ischemic heart disease and that the hormones adrenaline, noradrenaline and cortisol have a mediating role in this process.[2] In the first stage, the interaction of increased levels of these hormones leads to greater sensitivity of the heart. However, the sensitivity is not matched by the usual increase in dilation of the coronary arteries. At this point a functional but not a structural change has occurred. In the second stage there is a structural alteration to the arteries (coronary occlusion) which occurs when there have been repeated stress-induced increases in hormones. These repeated hormone increases lead to a number of changes in the arteries in both structure and function, culminating in coronary arteriosclerosis.

Many jobs require people to maintain acceptable levels of performance under difficult conditions. Workers who achieve this goal do so at a cost which is reflected in the secretion of hormones. This is because adrenaline, noradrenaline, cortisol, heart rate and blood pressure increase as a result of attempting to maintain job performance under conditions of job overload and underload. Where performance is maintained under difficult conditions, physiological cost increases and this may be accompanied by stress reactions and, in the long-term, ill-health.

In 1979 psychologist George Singer and I spent a research sabbatical in Sweden where we worked at the University of Stockholm with Bertil Gardell, Marianne Frankenhaeuser and her colleagues who were using hormone analysis to study occupational stress. On his return to Melbourne, Singer established the Brain-Behaviour Research Institute and, with Meredith Wallace at La Trobe University and Jack Bassett and at Macquarie University, we began a series of psychophysiological studies of occupational stress. Working together and independently we studied stress among factory and clerical workers, managers, shift-workers and aircraft cabin crew.

A study of female operators in a clothing factory found that workers subject to machine-controlled production processes had higher levels of adrenaline and noradrenaline than did workers on manually-operated machines which allowed more control over the work pace and greater utilisation of skills.[3] The results showed a hormonal increase for both manual and machine-controlled operators at the end of the working day. This is contrary to the normal twenty-four hour change pattern of the hormones in which levels should decline towards the end of the afternoon in preparation for rest and sleep during the evening. The hormonal patterns were reflected in the operators' questionnaire reports of an inability to unwind after work, which was the best predictor of job dissatisfaction and ill-health. The end of day arousal was much greater for the mechanised workers than for the manual workers, although this difference could only be detected by hormone analysis. None of the questionnaire responses revealed a difference which suggests that workers cannot explain to themselves or to others the origin of these feelings. In fact, a feature of this study was the high level of job satisfaction. The end-of-day hormonal levels in the clothing workers are probably a result of the fast pace originating in the incentive payment system (piece-rates). These results may constitute an early warning signal of the effects on health of mechanisation and payment-by-results systems.

The hormonal pattern of the clothing operators was then compared with that of women working in a munitions factory. Two similar levels of mechanisation were studied in both the clothing and munitions environments. While the clothing workers were paid by the piece, the munitions workers were paid a fixed wage. Results supported the prediction that the stress response, as measured by hormones in urine, would be greater under the piece-rate system than under the fixed-wage system. It is likely that working on a mechanised production system produces an increased stress response because of job overload. If so, stress is the result of mechanised work because, relative to manual work, operators would have difficulty in increasing the pace of production to take advantage of incentive payments. Workers would, therefore, have less control over production rates since they could modify only the input part of the production cycle. For this reason the higher stress levels were found among the workers who worked on the more highly mechanised systems on piece-rates.

In the 1980s, jet aircraft were travelling long distances across time zones. Understandably, aircraft crews wondered about the stress effects of long-distance flying and jet-lag. High physiological cost of work is obvious in the case of jet-lag due to the two types of stressors associated with long- distance flights at high altitudes over different time zones. First, there are the physical stressors encountered during the flight (noise, cabin pressure, low levels of oxygen and humidity). Second, there is the problem of adjusting to circadian rhythms and sleep patterns resulting from different time zones.

At the request of the union representing aircraft cabin attendants, Jack Bassett and I studied the stressful effects of two QANTAS crews on a flight from Sydney to Los Angeles and back again.[4] We reasoned that working on the flight was not likely to be associated with distress. While such factors as air turbulence, truculent passengers or general fatigue may influence feelings of well-being, it is more likely that distress, if experienced, would be due to jet-lag. Distress was assessed physiologically by urinary cortisol analysis and psychologically by mood ratings during a period which encompassed two days before, during and two days after the tour of duty. Two flights were studied with stopover times in Los Angeles of 56 and 84 hours in order to assess the different effects of adjustment to a new time zone.

The flight to Los Angeles did not involve an excessive physiological cost. While inadequate rest and dehydration were minor problems during the flight, they did not result in elevated levels of cortisol. But the period of time spent in Los Angeles was associated with increased levels of cortisol. It is possible that stressors associated with the incoming flight, such as fatigue and dehydration, may have contributed to the distress experienced during the stopover period. Such contribution, however, must have been small since after the return flight to Sydney all values rapidly returned to normal, even though the return flights appear to have been more stressful (based on cortisol levels) than the outward flights. The reason for the elevated cortisol levels and subjective reports of distress in Los Angeles is the disruption in circadian rhythm resulting from the change in night-day cycle. Individuals do not begin immediately to adjust to the alteration in day-night cycle and so there is a conflict between their biological clock and sensory information from the environment. The long-established circadian rhythms are out of phase with the existing environment. Such an asynchronism in the cycles associated with major bodily function is extremely stressful and requires an adaptation time in the order of several cycle durations. This is the essence of jet-lag. Such a disruption in circadian rhythm, as experienced in Los Angeles, would be carried over into the return flight and would explain the greater distress experienced on that flight. Relationships between cortisol excretion and mood ratings also revealed the influence of jet-lag. The stopover period in Los Angeles and the flight home were characterised by fatigue and lack of vitality. As the effects of jet-lag accumulated, vitality and vigour decreased. The stressful effects of the tour of duty dissipated within two days.

A related problem for workers is shift-work. George Singer and Meredith Wallace studied 900 electricity workers to establish the existence and nature of the difference between shift-workers and day-workers on factors relating to their quality of life.[5] Shift-workers reported more frequent occurrences of almost all health symptoms and experienced more 'nervous' problems. More shift-workers than day-workers reported receiving medical treatment for asthma, lung and breathing problems, stomach ulcers, arthritis and high blood pressure, but not for diabetes, cancer or heart disease. These health differences were not due to severe effects on a small proportion of shift-workers but rather moderate effects on a large proportion of the group studied. Shift-workers reported a more frequent use of laxatives, sleeping pills, pain-killers, cough medicines, tea, coffee, cigarettes and more dissatisfaction with their daily amount of sleep. In general, shift-workers perceived their health to be worse than others of the same age, worried more about their health and believed that work affects their health adversely. While shift-workers reported more interference to their family lives, especially in terms of the time available to spend with their families, they were not more likely to be divorced or separated from their spouses.

An unexpected finding was the response pattern of the shift-workers aged over 50 years. This group generally reported fewer problems than the other age groups and rarely differed significantly from the equivalent group of day-workers. This is in marked contrast to the 40-to 49-year old age group, where the largest differences between shift-workers and day-workers were found. The researchers interpreted the 50-year-old group as a survivor population, a group of workers relatively well adjusted to shift-work.

The researchers also compared day-workers with previous and current shift-workers. The results showed that on health issues previous shift-workers were intermediate between day-workers and current shift-workers, suggesting the possible influence of lasting health deficits due to exposure to shift-work. If shift- workers are a survivor population, then the previous shift-work group includes those who have failed to survive and the effects of shift-work may best be understood by an in-depth study of this group.

Wallace argued that the problem for shift-workers is that they attempt to work with inappropriate levels of hormones which may have a more immediate effect on health than prolonged exposure to stressful events. When adrenaline and noradrenaline levels are elevated, the individuals are aroused and alert. If this peak occurs when shift-workers are trying to rest, they will probably experience sleep problems and related disorders. Enzymes involved in the digestive processes of the body also have rhythms and digestive and gastric problems can occur if these are out of phase. Adrenaline and noradrenaline levels suggested that afternoon shift-workers were irritable and tense when they began their shift. Night shift-workers showed a marked drop in adrenaline in the middle of the shift indicating a sluggish state not conducive to optimal performance, and their flat noradrenaline levels suggested that this hormone rhythm had not adjusted: the levels were as low as typically found during the sleep period of day-workers. Both night and afternoon shift-workers left work with adrenaline levels as high as day-workers, suggesting they may have been too alert for sleep shortly after work.

Wallace was interested in determining appropriate patterns of hormone levels for well-adjusted shift-workers. She argued that if workers maintain the pattern that is normal for afternoon and night their hormonal responses are tuned to rest when they need to be alert. If the job they are doing is the same as the day-workers, then the most appropriate pattern of hormonal response is the same as found in day-workers who have no health or work-related problems. This requires a complete twelve-hour shift in bodily rhythms.

George Singer argued that an essential first premise from local research is that greater affluence of shift-workers may be a necessary but not a sufficient condition for an improvement in quality of life. More money may be essential for a higher material standard of living but it alone will not improve health and well-being. Shift-work is a problem which must be solved by workers and managers through critical discussion. Changes will be of two types: redesign of jobs and re-design of shift-workers' life styles. Traditionally, managers oppose the first solution and trade unionists oppose the second.[6]

Over the past forty years there has been considerable interest in the 12-hour shift roster where people work for two days (one day, one night) and have two days off. The benefits include: fewer working days and longer blocks of time off work; savings in time and cost of travel to and from work; elimination of afternoon shifts; more time with family at important periods; better quality of sleep; improved quality of working life; less accumulated fatigue; no increase in administrative costs; long- term improvements in health. In an Australian study Wallace found that four months after the introduction of a 12-hour roster prolonged working time did not produce increased fatigue. Performance of power station operators on a simulated task showed that measures of speed and accuracy during 12-hour shifts were superior to those during 8-hour shifts. After two years there was no evidence of increased operator errors, work-related injuries or accidents. She also found that quality of sleep was significantly better for the 12-hour shift-workers and that most workers reported considerable satisfaction with the new rosters.[7]

The QANTAS and shift-work studies used measures of stress hormones taken from urine, which are difficult to collect during work. Jack Bassett, Pam Marshall and I decided, therefore, to use measures of cortisol taken from saliva. We designed a study to evaluate a number of physiological measures of stress with a sample of bank managers attending a residential training course. The stressor involved was the preparation and delivery of a fifteen-minute public lecture. Measurement of various hormones, heart rate and blood pressure were taken five times during the day of the lecture and on the following day. Rates of adrenaline were significantly elevated immediately following, but not before, the lecture. Salivary cortisol levels were significantly increased both immediately before and after the lecture while blood pressure and heart rate were unchanged. We concluded that salivary cortisol levels are the measurement of choice in human studies of stress where individual stressors can be identified.[8] We then turned our attention to the study of stress among senior managers.

While there have been innumerable questionnaire studies of stress among managers, psychophysiological studies are virtually unknown. Normally, senior managers experience relatively high levels of job demands and high levels of job control which suggests that distress levels in senior managers will be, on average, lower than for many other job categories. Nonetheless, managers are exposed to a range of organisational stressors which may accumulate through the working week which suggests that a linear relationship exists between passage through the week and levels of distress. However, other psychological factors, such as the Australian 'Monday syndrome' in which individuals claim to experience distress at the thought of a week's work ahead of them, suggest that the relationship between period in the week and distress is a negative one. A third possibility is that distress levels will peak in mid-week, reflecting cumulative distress unrelieved by the prospect of immediate rest and relaxation.

A study of senior managers at Telecom (now Telstra) found that, relative to a rest-day baseline, cortisol excretion was significantly higher on Wednesday and on workday evenings.[9] Mood ratings showed that boredom and distress were associated with elevated cortisol levels and boredom was also associated with reported levels of illness. While we could not claim that certain managers were definitely at risk as far as stress-induced impairment of health is concerned, the elevated cortisol levels of the managers indicated an increased probability of stress-related disorders. The pattern of cortisol excretion through the working week offered no support to the advocates of the 'Monday syndrome'. Nor did our results support the cumulative distress model which predicted a linear relationship of increasing distress with increasing levels of cortisol throughout the week. We found that the relatively lower levels of cortisol on Friday afternoon suggested that the prospect of the weekend and the related diminution of work effort were associated with decreases in levels of distress. The relatively higher increases in cortisol on Wednesday pointed to a peak effort of work at mid-week some of which was experienced as distressing. Overall, we found that the changing patterns of cortisol through the week pointed to the situation-specific nature of the distress response. For example, high cortisol levels were associated with attendance at management meetings. Obviously, the workplace provided obstacles and opportunities that were quite different from the home environment.

In an era of increased awareness of occupational stress and the difficulty of assessment related thereto, this study might be seen as a model for researchers, managers and employees who would like to see a more objectively rigorous approach to the topic. Sadly, because of the high levels of litigation associated with the RSI debacle, managers are disinclined to sponsor such research for fear that it would trigger another round of courtroom battles. To my knowledge, our psychophysiological study of senior managers was the first and last one of its type in Australia.

9

MENTAL ILLNESS AS METAPHOR

Mind: Mythical entity with free will that replaces the soul as the spiritual centre of the manager.

In *Federal Broom Company v. Semlitch* (1964), the High Court of Australia confirmed that mental illness is a disease. An employee who had a previous history of schizophrenia had injured herself at work. Although she suffered from what turned out to be a side strain, she allegedly suffered from a 'delusion' that she had abdominal pain which incapacitated her for work.[1]

Cases of mental illness superimposed on physical injury are common in the workers' compensation area. There are many examples where employees suffer physical injury at work and although the effects of those injuries have disappeared, they maintain that they are incapacitated for work. Where it can be said that an employee has *genuinely* reacted in this way, the condition variously described as a functional overlay condition, or an *hysterical* condition, will be compensable if it results in incapacity for work and if it can be described as part of the natural consequences of a physical injury. However, legal experts in this field note that it is necessary to make a careful distinction between cases of unconscious and conscious malingering because the latter are not compensable.

French playwright Moliere (1622-1673) referred to functional overlay as malingering but Freud, under the influence of neurologist Jean-Martin Charcot (1825-1893), called it *hysteria* (derived from the Greek word for uterus), because he assumed it was a legitimate illness. Freud claimed that Charcot's work restored the dignity to hysterical individuals; and the sneering behaviour, which hysterics could reckon on meeting when they told their stories, was surrendered. Freud was delighted that they were no longer treated as malingerers and applauded Charcot for using his authority to legitimise hysterical phenomena. Because of the unchallenged authority of Charcot, hysterics were no longer diagnosed and treated as malingerers. While Charcot acknowledged that malingering is a feature of hysteria, he laid it down that hysterical patients *did not know* they were malingering. Malingerers consciously imitate illness; hysterics unconsciously imitate illness. It was, therefore, the task of psychiatrists to decide whether patients were consciously or unconsciously imitating illness. How could this be done?

As there are no criteria by which such a judgement can be made, it is unsurprising that psychiatrists declared that not only is hysteria an illness, but so too is malingering. They argue that there is no way to tell the difference between a person who is ill and one who pretends to be ill: both are ill. This curious line of thinking effectively denies the ability and willingness of people to imitate illness, which is absurd. In 1924 the man who invented schizophrenia, Eugen Bleuler, asserted that those who simulate insanity cleverly are psychopaths and some are actually insane. The ability to simulate illness, therefore, does not prove that patients are mentally healthy and responsible for their actions. In other words, those who simulate insanity are insane!

Claims for compensation based on functional overlay are not automatically accepted by Australian courts. An example of a 'compensation neurosis' that was not compensable is provided in *Kirkpatrick v. Commonwealth of Australia* (1985).[2] An employee sustained an injury at work, was discharged by his doctor as being fit to return to work, but chose not to do so. Psychiatric evidence supported the diagnosis of compensation neurosis which was the result of the employee's view that he had been unfairly treated by his employer. Consequently, he believed that he continued to have a physical problem which was related to the injury. His compensation neurosis developed after his claim for compensation had been rejected. The fact that the employee thought his disability arose out of his work, and was therefore compensable, may have been potent factors in the development of his neurosis. But, the judge noted, these were 'thoughts in his mind'. They did not mean that his employment actually was a contributing factor in the development of his neurosis.

Whenever 'mind' is brought into a discussion of health and well-being, there is dangerous tendency to treat this abstract noun as if it is a concrete noun. In this way, we commit what philosopher Gilbert Ryle calls a 'category-error', where we represent the facts of mental life as if they belong to one logical category when they actually belong to another. By treating mind as a thing, like the brain, we fall into the trap of assigning brain-like qualities to 'it'. We are faced with two possibilities: the mind is a spiritual 'substance'; or there is no such thing as a mind. In either case, the mind is not the brain. If people insist that the mind is the brain, then we have a redundant concept.

Today 'mind' functions as both noun and verb. In *The Meaning of Mind*, psychiatrist Thomas Szasz points out that before the sixteenth century people did not have minds – they had souls – and 'mind' was used only as a verb ('mind the shop'). But with the gradual decline of religious dogma, the use of soul declined in proportion as the use of 'mind' increased. In short, the religious 'soul' gave way to the quasi-scientific 'mind'. As 'mind' came from the Latin *mens*, which means intention or will, it is an activity, not a thing. 'Mind' cannot, therefore, be a thing in the brain, or anywhere else. And obviously there can be nothing 'in the mind' just as there can be nothing in the activity called 'running'. When we say that we have thoughts, feelings, beliefs and values 'in the mind' we have committed a category error. In short, we have no mind even though we are minded in that we engage in activities such as minding a step, minding a shop, or minding ourselves.

As there is no entity called 'mind' we identify minding with thinking, which is talking to oneself. Socrates said that he described thinking as discourse, as a statement pronounced silently to oneself. Minding is, therefore, the ability to attend and adapt to one's environment by talking to others and to oneself. Because we attribute this ability to intelligent beings, minding implies moral agency which means that we are thinking beings, willing and able to function as responsible members of society. There is then an obvious connection between minding, thinking, talking, and since reason is a function of all three activities, so too is unreason.

If there is no such thing as mind, there can be no illnesses of the mind except in the metaphorical sense in which a course of action is 'ill-advised'. Mental illness is, therefore, a myth. And if mental illness is a myth, mental health is also.

In *The Myth of Mental Illness*, Szasz revealed the problematic nature of mental illness, which can be demonstrated by simple deductive logic:

1. Illness affects the body (by definition).
2. The 'mind' is not a bodily organ (either because it is spiritual or because it does not exist);
3. Therefore, the mind cannot be, or become, ill (except metaphorically).
4. Therefore, mental illness is a myth.
5. If mind is really brain (as popularly believed),
6. Then mental illnesses are really brain illnesses.
7. Brain illnesses are diagnosed objectively on the basis of medical signs,
8. But no mental illness has been diagnosed objectively on the basis of medical signs (they are diagnosed subjectively according to moral criteria),
9. Therefore, mental illness is still a myth.

When Szasz says that mental illness is a myth, he does not deny the behaviours to which the so-called mental illnesses are applied. People have always acted in bizarre, weird, 'mad' ways that upset, annoy or offend others, but they have not always been called 'mentally ill'. But are such people, literally or metaphorically, ill?

Economies and jokes are sometimes said to be 'sick'. Rational people recognise the metaphor and do not conclude that economies or jokes suffer from cancer or need chemotherapy. A metaphor is a figure of speech in which a term is applied to something to which it is not literally applicable, in order to suggest a resemblance. In other words, a metaphor is not literally true, which means it is false.

To recognise a metaphor we have to understand the literal meaning of a word. So we recognise 'sick' or 'ill' when the word describes a person with an illness of the body, such as multiple sclerosis. Illnesses of the brain are therefore legitimate illnesses; illnesses of the mind are not.

If mental illnesses are undiagnosed brain illnesses, they are not mental illnesses and we do not need to concern ourselves with two types of disease: bodily and mental. But body/mind dualism has such a hold over people that it is assumed that we 'have' bodies and minds and that both can be ill. But here confusion obtains because many psychiatrists, psychologists and government bureaucrats maintain that 'mental illnesses are like all other illnesses'. If true, then there are only bodily illnesses and so-called mental patients retain all their normal rights and responsibilities. If mental patients are really legitimate medical patients, they can reject hospitalisation and medical treatment and they cannot plead incompetence in courts of law. That we treat people with bodily illnesses differently from those with so-called mental illnesses is obvious from these examples; and raises important questions about the political significance and advantages of maintaining the distinction between the two forms of illness.

The upshot of this psychiatric propaganda is that today it is considered insensitive in the extreme to treat individuals who have been labelled 'mentally ill' as if they were not ill. We are told repeatedly that we 'now know' that such people are (mentally) ill. This illogical view rests on a simple error: that of confusing what is literally true with what is metaphorical.

Nowadays, individuals who act in ways that annoy, upset or offend others, or who upset themselves, are likely to be diagnosed with a mental illness. Since behaviour that annoys, offends or upsets others is judged according to a standard of values, diagnoses of mental illnesses are based on moral criteria. Thus we confuse medicine with morals. Whereas bodily illnesses are what people *have*, mental illnesses are what *they do or say*. While there can be treatments and cures for a bodily illnesses, there can be no treatments or cures for mental illnesses. It follows that so-called mental health problems are not medical but moral, political, social dilemmas which cannot be solved by therapeutic means.

It is axiomatic that if something is impossible in logic it is impossible in every other way, technically, empirically and scientifically. Because combining 'mental' and 'illness' produces an oxymoron, the debate should end here. But history tells us that people are rarely persuaded by logic. It is necessary, therefore, to analyse the empirical status of mental illness which, as we shall see, is also profoundly problematic.

Legitimate bodily illnesses are to be found listed in books of pathology where illness, or disease, is defined in terms of functional or structural abnormalities of the body. One of the best known authoritative books of pathology – *Robbins Basic Pathology* – is clear on the matter. Pathology is the study of diseases. It involves the investigation of the causes of disease and the associated changes at the levels of cells, tissues, and organs which in turn give rise to signs and symptoms. To render diagnoses and guide therapy in clinical practice, pathologists identify changes in the gross or microscopic appearance (morphology) of cells and tissues, and biochemical alterations in fluids. In short, illness affects bodies.

Books of pathology enumerate diseases that have been discovered and confirmed by objective tests. They do not include mental illnesses among the legitimate diseases. Diagnosis of real disease is based on the presence of medical signs which are, by definition, objective and without which diagnoses are putative.

For a catalogue of 'diseases of the mind', a book of pathology will not help: another book is required. It is a best seller and has become something of a psychiatric bible. A product of the American Psychiatric Association (APA), it is misleadingly titled *Diagnostic and Statistical Manual of Mental Disorders* (DSM). The title is misleading in two ways: there are few statistics therein; and the term 'mental disorder' is a euphemism for mental illness. First published as a slim volume of 130 pages in 1952, the fifth edition of more than 900 pages was published in 2013.

DSM-I reflected the dominance of the psychoanalytic perspective and while DSM-II included few theoretical changes, the times were indeed a-changing. By the late 1970s it was clear that the days of the dominance of the psychoanalytic perspective were numbered, at least as far as the authors of DSM-III were concerned. This group, led by psychiatrist Robert Spitzer, was determined to return psychiatry to its home in medicine. Thus began the progressive medicalisation of everyday behaviour, and especially misbehaviour, which has dominated psychiatry ever since.

In 1976 Spitzer and psychologist Jean Endicott drafted a new definition of mental disorder and presented it to the conference of the APA. There was uproar. Psychologists were particularly upset with the assertion that 'mental disorders are a subset of medical disorders'. The president of the American Psychological Association, Theodore Blau, objected in the strongest terms. He pointed out that of the 17 major diagnostic classes, at least ten have no known organic aetiology and many are obviously acquired through learning experiences. These were clearly not medical conditions. In his reply, Spitzer wrote that he wanted to make it clear to his profession that DSM-III will help psychiatry move closer to the rest of medicine. Blau replied in equally strong terms that DSM-III is more of a political position paper for the American Psychiatric Association than a scientifically-based classification system. In the end the statement did not appear in DSM-III but the battle lines had been drawn.[3]

The debate between the psychiatrists and psychologists was never about logic or empirical evidence. If it had been, there would be no need to quibble over the meaning of 'mental disorder'. Empirically, if mental disorders are medical disorders they are in the same category as multiple sclerosis. As there is no empirical evidence to support this hypothesis and insofar as mental disorders are diagnosed on subjective criteria, 'scientific' psychiatrists and psychologists might be expected to dispense with the idea of mental disorder. Yet they continue to involve themselves in conceptual muddles and base rhetoric. And the spectacle of psychiatrists and psychologists fighting with each other over the meaning of such a fundamental term should raise alarm bells in the public arena since it indicates that all is not well with the psychiatric and psychological professions and DSM. Given that this psychiatric bible is so influential and is used to justify the mass drugging of human beings, including millions of children worldwide, it is surely cause for concern that its authors cannot agree on basic definitions.

This acrimonious debate was about power, prestige and control of the language of illness. If psychiatrists ignore valid logical and empirical objections and convince themselves and the public that mental disorders are medical illnesses, the claim that they require medical treatment follows naturally. This has the consequence that behavioural issues are treated as medical illnesses which require the services of doctors of medicine. It is unsurprising that psychologists would object to the medicalisation of behavioural issues. Yet they continue to work actively alongside psychiatrists in condemning people to medical treatment for non-medical conditions. *Cui bono?*

We might be tempted at this point to say 'a plague on both your houses'. Mental disorders, such as gambling or hoarding, are clearly not medical illnesses, because they cannot be diagnosed objectively according to medical criteria. If they were so diagnosed they would be, by definition, bodily illnesses. So the psychologists are right on this point. But they mislead the public when they assert that there are medical disorders *and* mental disorders. Had they refused to use the term 'mental disorder' and replaced it with '(mis) behaviour', they would have avoided the notorious problem of mind-body dualism. But they would have fallen foul of the DSM classification system which dominates their profession. Without a classification system, psychologists believe that their field lacks scientific legitimacy.

DSM is a book of political and professional agreements which lack logical and empirical support. The history of science tells us that agreements do not necessarily reflect reality since scientists have agreed on propositions which are false. For example, homosexuality was accepted as a mental illness by the authors of DSM-I and rejected by the authors of DSM-III. That experts agree about a topic is no reason to believe that their consensus is valid: validity is concerned with truth not agreement.

The first definition of mental disorder appears in DSM-III. It was not intended to guide diagnostic decisions but to fill an embarrassing void in earlier editions of the manual. DSM-III defines mental disorder as an 'internal dysfunction' which is 'in the individual' thereby making it compatible with the medical view that it is an illness. Clearly, 'dysfunction' implies some internal abnormality which causes the mental disorder, yet the authors do not see fit to offer a definition of 'dysfunction'. The DSM definition requires that a mental disorder has harmful effects to the individual: distress; disability; or pain. But as these occur in a social setting, external factors are thereby introduced into the medical model. The idea that mental disorders are *communications*, stemming from unsatisfactory relationships with people, is rejected.

Because of the conceptual confusion about what constitutes a mental disorder, DSM's clumsy definition allowed many 'disorders' to be moved into (or out of) the manual simply by putting them to a vote of APA members. In this way, homosexuality was removed from, and ADHD was added to, DSM in 1973 and 1987 respectively.

DSM-III was published in 1980. The 150 pages of DSM-II had blown out to 500 pages of mental disorders. When psychoanalytic therapy was used with clients, specific diagnoses were relatively unimportant. This changed with the publication of DSM-III, where clients were transformed into patients, psychotherapists into doctors of medicine, and talking therapy into medical treatment. And there was no shortage of diagnostic categories: more than 270 categories filled the pages, including Post-Traumatic Stress Disorder, which made its psychiatric debut.

The medical approach to psychiatry is based on important relationships with pharmaceutical companies and medical insurance companies. Parading the hypothesis of chemical imbalances in the brain as an established fact, psychiatrists prescribe medication which allegedly re-balances the wayward chemicals. Yet, most of the mental illnesses in DSM-III and later editions do not present with objective signs. Those that do are called 'organic mental disorders' because they combine a medical condition with abnormal behaviour. In other words, DSM is mainly concerned with behavioural issues. A small number of conditions of known aetiology are listed, including the vascular brain disease known as 'Alzheimer's', but it is called a mental condition presumably because it affects short-term memory. Schizophrenia and affective disorders (manic-depression) are defined as medical rather than psychological conditions.

By 2000, conceptual ambiguities had not improved. Having admitted that no definition adequately specifies precise boundaries for the concept of 'mental disorder', the authors of DSM-IV-R admitted that although the manual is titled *Diagnostic and Statistical Manual of Mental Disorders*, the term 'mental disorder' unfortunately implies a distinction between mental and physical disorders that is a reductionistic anachronism of mind/body dualism. And so it is. But the authors then embrace this dualism when they assert that a compelling literature suggests that there is much that is 'physical' in 'mental' disorders and much that is 'mental' in 'physical' disorders. Astonishingly, they admit that the problem raised by the term 'mental' disorders has been much clearer than its solution and unfortunately the term persists in the title of DSM-IV because the authors have not found an appropriate substitute.

Had they been logical rather than political in their thinking they would have concluded that there are bodily illnesses and there are (mis)behaviours (misleadingly called 'mental disorders'). They could then have dispensed with 'mind' and 'mental' entirely. But this would raise embarrassing questions about why they call misbehaviours illnesses which require medical treatment. Bearing in mind that DSM lists 'Academic Disorder' and 'Mathematics Disorder' as mental illnesses, it is easy to see how behaviours which disappoint, annoy or offend others have been turned into mental disorders and treated with drugs.

Professional and public criticism of DSM accelerated after the publication of DSM-IV and came to a head before and after the appearance of DSM-5. Predictably, psychologists criticised the medicalisation of moral behaviour, while members of the public expressed concern about the fact that more than sixty percent of the DSM task force had financial relationships with pharmaceutical companies. The vagueness of definitions also attracted widespread criticism.

The authors of DSM-5 admit that although no definition can capture all aspects of all mental disorders in the manual, the following elements are required. A mental disorder is characterised by clinical disturbance in an individual's cognition, emotion, or behaviour that reflects a dysfunction in the psychological, biological, or developmental processes underlying mental functioning. Mental disorders are associated with significant distress or disability. A culturally approved response to a common stressor or loss, such as death of a loved one, is not a mental disorder. Socially deviant behaviour and conflicts that are primarily between the individual and society are not mental disorders unless the deviance or conflict results from a dysfunction in the individual. Use of DSM-5 to diagnose a mental disorder by nonclinical, nonmedical, or insufficiently trained individuals is not advised.

DSM's definition of mental disorder begs more questions than it answers. Applying such words as 'disturbance' and 'dysfunction' to so-called mental disorders raise normative questions about the criteria that psychiatrists use to determine the degree to which socially deviant behaviour is a rational expression of dissatisfaction with society's values or the result of an illness. How does a psychiatrist distinguish eccentricity or social protest from mental illness? If 'significant distress' is the important criterion, there is no limit to the number of potential mental illnesses since individuals can be distressed about anything.

Included in DSM-5 are the following mental disorders: antisocial personality; avoidant personality; binge-eating; caffeine use; child maltreatment and neglect; gambling; hair-pulling; hoarding; illness anxiety; internet gaming; jealousy; narcissistic personality; obesity; paedophilia; partner neglect; premature ejaculation; relational problems; rumination; and written expression problems.

In 1992, the Australian Health Ministers' Advisory Council established a national policy for mental health. This policy aims, in part, to reduce the 'negative' impact of mental illness on the community. To this end, government departments and community groups have been exhorting the public to accept the reality of mental illness and to avoid stigmatising and discriminating against the mentally ill. A government-sponsored study recommended that the following messages must be communicated to the public: 'mental illness is an illness like any other'; 'early treatment is important'; 'willpower alone is not enough'; and importantly, 'it is not their fault or their choice'. The study lamented the considerable confusion about which conditions are mental illnesses and which are physical illnesses. It concluded that this confusion is a significant concern because, to the extent that confusion occurs, there will be inappropriate assumptions made about the characteristics of mental illness.[4]

Given the wealth of published concerns about the status of mental illness, researchers were determined to draw attention to the widespread ignorance of and confusion about mental illness and its alleged causes. They bolstered this strategy with the view that stress is the main cause of mental problems and stress management the key defence. Of the more than 1200 Australians sampled, 70% were characterised in the report as 'rednecks' because their views are 'conservative, prejudiced and ill-informed'. The most 'tolerant' sectors of the community are females, under 25s, white-collar workers, and the university educated. Females are judged to be better informed than males about mental illness because they can name more conditions and report more exposure to and sympathy for the mentally ill.

Managers hold opinions about mental illness which are 'relatively unfavourable and discriminatory'. While managers support educational opportunities for the mentally ill and reject the view that they are unreliable or a negative influence on staff morale, they are criticised because they believe supervision is essential for mentally ill employees. The negative characterisation of managers appears to be based on the finding that 86% of the 77 managers sampled agreed that disclosing mental illness would ruin an individual's chance of getting a job. Indeed, in interviews conducted with 'consumers' (those with a history of mental illness), it was admitted that in order to get a job 'the usual strategy is to lie' to potential employers. One can hardly blame managers (or anyone else) for their 'negative' attitudes when faced with such a contentious and tendentious subject.

If we expand our thinking beyond the government rhetoric, three influential views about the nature of mental illness are encountered in the literature: biological; environmental; and strategic. The biological view assumes that mental illness is an illness of the brain, probably caused by chemical imbalances therein. The environmental view assumes that mental illness is dysfunctional behaviour caused by adverse social conditioning. Some proponents of this view (behaviourists) deny the existence of mind and therefore of mental illness; others (cognitivists) assume an abnormal state of the mind/brain caused by inadequate cognitive coping with stressors. The strategic view assumes that personal conduct is rule-following and meaningful and that abnormal conduct can be analysed as if it is a game in which individuals adopt roles (patient, stoic) and follow rules to achieve their goals. On this view, mental illness is a label used by some participants in a game to stigmatise those whose behaviour annoys or offends them. Alternatively, individuals may label themselves as mentally ill to escape from an intolerable situation or to gain personal rewards, especially sympathy from others.

My 1999 study of 917 Australian managers revealed the existence of these three perspectives.[5] When asked about mental illness, about 25% of the sample endorsed the *strategic* view, agreeing that, for example, mental illness is: a strategy employed to gain a reward (19%); a label for moral problems (24%); a way of escaping unpleasantness (44%); coercion concealed as loss of control (30%); eccentric behaviour (41%); not an illness but a way of acting (34%).

About 50% endorsed the environmental view agreeing that mental illness is caused by: problems in childhood (61%); domestic problems (42%); social conditioning (55%); or poor parenting (28%). 66% agreed that mental illness is an illness of the mind.

Roughly 44% supported the *biological* view agreeing that mental illness is caused by: chemical imbalance in the brain (76%); hormone problems (53%); or an inherited condition (50%). Following the government line, 54% agreed that mental illness is an illness of the brain and 46% said that it is like any other physical illness.

Clearly, there is a degree of overlap in attitudes about mental illness. Males preferred the strategic view while females were the stronger advocates for the biological and environmental views. None of these views is consistent with the notion of mental illness, however, since the biological view insists that mental illness is physical illness, the environmental view emphasises behavioural abnormalities, and the strategic view denies the existence of mental illness.

With the authority of DSM to support them, governments around the world have promoted the view that 'mental illnesses are like all other illnesses.' Governments, ably supported by psychiatrists and psychologists, have used the idea of 'mental health literacy' to describe people who promote an illness ideology. Many attempts to reduce prejudice against the mentally ill have been based on the assumption that if individuals are ill their behaviour is beyond their control and they cannot be held responsible for it. However, psychologist John Read reported studies from seventeen countries which show that citizens have steadfastly resisted this propaganda, preferring to attribute mental illness to practical and moral problems in living. He argues that the 'mental illness is an illness like any other' propaganda ignores the large body of research evidence that biogenetic explanations actually fuel fear and prejudice.[6]

The DHA authors acknowledge that the causes of mental illness are complex, which is true since if there is no mental illness there is no cause of that illness. But then they present speculation as fact by asserting that the causes of mental illness *probably* represent an interaction between genetics, personality, and life experience. This is psychobabble parading as scientific fact. Not satisfied with this speculation they add that studies *suggest* that there is often a biological change associated with mental illness, such as a change in the neurotransmitter levels in the brain, or variations in brain activity as shown by imaging techniques. The use of such words as 'probably' and 'suggest' gives the game away. Such words would not be needed if their statements were based on scientifically proven facts.

Neurologist Fred Baughman, who actually discovered a (real) neurological illness, notes that not one mental illness has been discovered: they have all been invented.[7] In English there are 'success' verbs, such as 'discover', because discovering something is an achievement: one cannot discover something that does not exist. 'Invent', however, is not a success verb since one can invent something that does not exist. Brain illnesses are discovered; mental illnesses are invented: they are metaphorical illnesses at best, naked emperors at worst.

Despite these professional opinions, government bureaucrats and the psychiatric and psychological communities continue to promote the myth of chemical imbalance. The DHA *Response Ability* website states that research *suggests* that certain substances in the brain are involved in the development of the disorder (schizophrenia), particularly the neurotransmitter dopamine. Some families show a genetic vulnerability to the illness, *perhaps* by passing on a gene which is related to dopamine levels. Yet researchers too numerous to mention have stated that a sustained search for neurochemical abnormalities in schizophrenia patients has drawn a blank.[8]

In ethics and law, people are regarded as moral agents if they are answerable for their conduct. Being responsible is, therefore, a type of 'minding' and assumes that people can communicate to others and to themselves. When we are in a moral relationship with others we talk of responsibility; when we are in a relationship with ourselves we talk of conscience. In short, Thomas Szasz sees conscience as a particular kind of self-conversation, the person's inner dialogue concerning the goodness or badness of its own conduct. Since talking to others and to oneself is a voluntary act, responsibility can be seen as the paradigmatic self-conversation. The concepts 'right' and 'wrong', 'responsibility' and 'mind' should be treated as a single entity. Conversely, the view that 'mind' is an entity, such as brain, is not a scientific fact. How could it be? Its purpose is to enable individuals to evade responsibility for their actions. The language of minding entails responsibility; the language of mind/brain protects people from the difficulties of facing up to their responsibilities.

The myth of the mind generated the myth of mental illness, in which there is a certain irony. The mind was to be the source of human freedom and responsibility; mental illness is the source of un-freedom and non-responsibility. The mind is a metaphor and mental illness is metaphorical illness which has been literalised. A consequence of such literalising is the progressive undermining of personal responsibility. If the twin notions of mental illness and non-responsibility are rejected, then the 'mentally ill' will be given back their freedom, dignity and self-responsibility.

If mental illness is a myth, so too is mental health. Indeed, if 'mental health' means anything at all, it means it is a *moral* condition: the result of facing life courageously, accepting its tragic nature and creating autonomy for oneself. No one automatically develops mental health without making significant and often difficult choices. If mental health is the result of people's choices, they are responsible for maintaining it. Mental health depends on the brain only to the extent that all behaviour requires a healthy brain. Mental health is not a condition but an achievement.

EPILOGUE

In 2007, psychology professor Kevin R. Murphy compiled a list of the greatest successes and failures of organisational psychology.[1] He based his list on his personal experience of the field and on the opinions of his colleagues. The list of successes includes: the growth of the field; the scientist-practitioner model; measurement and statistical analysis; and meta-analysis of cognitive tests. His 'misses' or failures represent a serious indictment on the profession and cast doubt on the validity of at least two of his 'hits'.

1. Meta-analyses of the validity of personality tests as predictors of job performance have shown that 'the sort of broad personality traits that were the focus of meta-analytic research in the 1990s and beyond generally show quite low levels of predictive ability; and they look good only in comparison with previous assumptions that showed no validity whatsoever.

2. While emotional intelligence consultants are doing a booming business, 'most of the attention-grabbing claims regarding EQ are either exaggerated or completely wrong. There is little credible evidence that emotional intelligence is an important or unique predictor of performance, or that it is more important than cognitive ability in predicting *any* broad

criteria. While there are some potentially interesting ideas in the EQ literature, the concept has not lived up to the hype.'

3. 360-Degree feedback is another 'hot' topic in management. Naïve advocates promote the view that multiple parties should be involved in providing feedback on performance. Murphy points to the obvious fact that performance ratings from different sources almost always contradict each other. 'These [360-degree] systems seem to be built for failure. They will typically produce discrepant feedback and will provide users with solid reasons to ignore much of the negative feedback they receive.'

4. Maslow's hierarchy of needs remains one of the most popular theories in the management psychological literature. Yet, Murphy acknowledges that none of its key ideas has received empirical support, nor is it likely that such support will be forthcoming in future research. Weaknesses of the Maslow model have been well known for over forty years, but the model remains popular. 'Like creationism and intelligent design theories, Maslow's model seems to be sustained mainly on the basis of people's assumptions about what *should* be true, not by the evidence. It is well past time to drop this relic from I/O psychology textbooks.'

5. Another popular topic – organisational climate – is based on a metaphor. Do organisations have climates, or do people talk as if they do? Can we actually take the temperature of an organisation as some writers have suggested? 'Organisational climate' is like 'emotional intelligence': both terms are metaphorical, conceptually inadequate and

empirically unsupported. After years of fruitless research, their days are, or should be, over.

Industrial and organisational psychologists, Murphy noted, continue to act as servants of power. Indeed, those who listen to psychomanagers cannot have any doubt that their aim is to understand and control human behaviour. Human beings are to be 'constructed' so as to fit the bureaucratic order of society. Personality psychology is to be the agent of the economic bureaucracy in creating a modern synthesis between itself and the psychological structure of its recruits.

Underlying the behaviour of psychomanagers, and the psychologists' aim of helping them control the behaviour of colleagues, is the unexpressed faith that an increase in managerial power is sufficient to solve organisational problems. The history of management is alone sufficient to cast doubt on the wisdom of placing much faith in this assumption. Power concentrated in managerial groups becomes relatively unresponsive to human values since there is no internal dynamic which guarantees that its use shall be benign. The powers of individuals, on the other hand, are to an unprecedented degree under the direction of managers rather than under the direction of an ethic based on the value of human beings as such, and the first care of managers is so to direct their colleagues as to protect and enlarge their own power. People today find themselves in the position of those who cannot avoid participating in the generation of formidable amounts of managerial power, but are unable to devise adequate means for its control. They are therefore unable to secure themselves against the possibility of its being used against them. This is especially the case when psychologists become servants of power and use their skills to manipulate and control people.

NOTES AND REFERENCES

Chapter 1: A Weird Country

1. M. Franklin, *Joseph Furphy: The Legend of a Man and his Book*, Rushcutters Bay: Halstead Press, 1944/2011, p. 7.
2. D.H. Lawrence, *The Letters of D.H. Lawrence*, Vol. 4, (eds. W. Roberts, J. Boulton & E. Mansfield), Cambridge: Cambridge University Press, 1987, pp. 263-264.
3. T. Collins, *Such is Life*, Hawthorn: Lloyd O'Neil, 1970, p. 371.
4. H. Heseltine, 'The Australian Image: The Literary Heritage', in C. Semmler, (ed.), *Twentieth Century Australian Literary Criticism*, Melbourne: Oxford University Press, 1967, p. 101.
5. N. Lindsay, 'Australia and Australians', in K. Wingrove (ed.), *Norman Lindsay: On Art, Life and Literature*, St. Lucia: University of Queensland Press, 1990, pp. 85-89.
6. B. O'Reilly, *Green Mountains*, South Yarra: Lloyd O'Neil, 1940/1983, pp. 96-97.
7. Quoted in D. Jones & B. Andrews, 'Australian Humour', in L. Hergenhan (ed.), *New Literary History of Australia*, Ringwood: Penguin, 1988, p. 67.
8. Quoted in G.A. Wilkes, *The Stockyard and the Croquet Lawn: Literary Evidence for Australian Cultural Development*, London: Edward Arnold, 1981, p.142.

9. L. Murray, *The Quality of Sprawl: Thoughts about Australia*, Sydney: Duffy & Snellgrove, 1999, pp. 1-2.

Chapter 2: Managers and Mates

1. D. Horne, *The Lucky Country*: Harmondsworth: Penguin, 1971, pp. 71-73.
2. H. Stretton, 'The Quality of Leading Australians', *Daedalus*, 1985, 114, pp. 197-230.
3. R.J. Chambers, 'First Australian Management Diploma Course', *Manufacturing Management*, 1948, 3, 5, pp. 145-147.
4. H. Craig, T. Pauling & I. Wearne, 'Personnel Management in the N.S.W. Public Service', *Public Administration*, 1949, 8, 143-161.
5. W.J. Byrt & P.R. Masters, *The Australian Manager*, Melbourne: Sun Books, 1974, p. 65.
6. G. Renwick, *A Fair Go for All: Australian/American Interactions* (eds. R. Smart & D. Henderson), Yarmouth, ME: Intercultural Press, 1991.
7. R. Spillane, 'Attitudes of Business Executives and Union Leaders to Industrial Relations', *Journal of Industrial Relations*, 1980, 22, 3, pp. 317-326.
8. G. Henderson, 'Not Much Enterprise in Karpin Report', *Sydney Morning Herald*, 16 May 1995, p. 13.
9. F. Emery, 'Karpin Taskforce Manages to Get Confused', *Business Review Weekly*, 24 July 1995, p. 72.

10. J. Martin & J. Ray, 'Anti-authoritarianism: An Indicator of Pathology', *Australian Journal of Psychology*, 1972, 24, 1, pp. 13-18.

Chapter 3: The Great Debate

1. P.F. Drucker, *Adventures of a Bystander*, London: William Heinemann, 1979, p.287.
2. P.F. Drucker, 'The Coming Rediscovery of Scientific Management', in *Towards the Next Economics and Other Essays*, London: Heinemann, 1981, pp. 96-106.
3. A. Carey, 'The Hawthorne Studies: A Radical Criticism, *American Sociological Review*, 1967, 32, p. 416.
4. K. Lewin, R. Lippitt & K. White, 'Patterns of Aggressive Behaviour in Experimentally Created 'Social Climates', *Journal of Sociology*, 1939, 10, pp. 271-299.
5. A. Carey, 'Industrial Psychology and Sociology in Australia,' in P. Boreham, A. Pemberton & P. Wilson (eds.), *The Professions in Australia: A Critical Appraisal*, St. Lucia: University of Queensland Press, 1976, p. 238.
6. For details and references see R. Lansbury & R. Spillane, *Organisational Behaviour: The Australian Context* (2nd ed.), Melbourne: Longman Cheshire, 1991, pp. 101-105.
7. P.F. Drucker, 'Have Employee Relations Policies Had the Desired Effects?' *American Management Association, Personnel Series*, 1950, 134, p. 7.

8. P.F. Drucker, *Managing for the Future*, Oxford: Butterworth-Heinemann, 1992, p. 103.
9. P.F. Drucker, 'The Unfashionable Kierkegaard', in *The New Markets and Other Essays*, London: Heinemann, 1971, pp. 44-58.

Chapter 4: Motivation and Manipulation

1. S. Andreski, *Social Sciences as Sorcery*, Harmondsworth: Penguin, 1974, p. 69.
2. For details and references see, R.D. Lansbury & R. Spillane, *Organisational Behaviour: The Australian Context*, Melbourne: Longman Cheshire, 1991, pp. 255-279.
3. D. Clutterbuck & G. Bickerstaffe, 'Where Have all the Gurus Gone?' *International Management*, January 1982, pp. 12-15.
4. P.F. Drucker, 'Behind Japan's Success', *Towards the Next Economics and Other Essays*, London: Heinemann, 1981, pp. 164-180.

Chapter 5: The Personality Cult

1. R. Kramar et al., *Human Resource Management: Strategy, People, Performance*, North Ryde: McGraw-Hill, 2014, p. 270.
2. M.R. Barrick & M.K. Mount, 'The Big Five Personality Dimensions and Job Performance: A Meta-Analysis', *Personnel Psychology*, 1991, 44, pp. 1-26.
3. Details of this case can be found in E. Alderman & C. Kennedy, *The Right to Privacy*, New York: Alfred A. Knopf, 1995, pp. 277-290.
4. F. Marks & B. McLean, *Workers Compensation Law and Practice in New South Wales*, (3rd ed.), North Ryde: CCH Australia, 1992, p. 256.

Chapter 6: Unintelligent Intelligence

1. L. Spillane, 'Language and Values: Communication Styles of Australian Pubic Service Managers', *Australian Journal of Public Administration*, 1994, 53, 1, pp. 63-66.

Chapter 7: The RSI Debacle

1. Workers Compensation Commission of NSW, *Compensation Reports New South Wales*, Vol XLVII, Government Printer, NSW, 1973, p. iv.
2. J. Mathews & N. Calabrese, 'Guidelines for the Prevention of Repetitive Strain Injury (RSI),' *Health and Safety Bulletin*, 1982, 18, pp. 1-33.
3. L. Deves & R. Spillane, 'Occupational Health, Stress and Work Organisation in Australia,' *International Journal of Health Services*, 19, 2, pp. 351-363.
4. M. Quinlan & P. Bohle, *Managing Occupational Health and Safety in Australia*, Melbourne: Macmillan, 1991, p. 126.
5. R. Spillane & L. Deves, 'Psychological Correlates of RSI Reporting', *Journal of Occupational Health &Safety – Australia & New Zealand*, 1988, 4, pp. 21-27.
6. B. Hocking, 'Epidemiological Aspects of "Repetition Strain Injury" in Telecom Australia', *Medical Journal of Australia*, 1987, 147, pp. 218-222.
7. For detailed references see R. Spillane, 'Medicalising Work Behaviour: The Case of Repetition Strain Injury, *Asia Pacific Journal of Human Resources*, 2008, 46, 1, pp. 85-99.

Chapter 8: Stress and Controllability

1. R. Karasek, 'Job Socialisation and Job Strain: The Implications of Two Related Psychological Mechanisms for Job Design', in B. Gardell & G. Johansson (eds.), *Working Life: A Social Science Contribution to Work Reform*, Chichester: Wiley, 1981, pp. 75-94.
2. J.R. Bassett, 'Psychological Stress and the Coronary Artery in Ischaemic Heart Disease', in S. Kalsner (ed.), *The Coronary Artery*, London: Croom Helm, 1982, pp. 474-500.
3. N. Romas, et al., 'Measuring Physiological Stress Responses: The Effects of Factors in the Work Environment on Urinary Catecholamine Responses', *Journal of Occupational Health & Safety – Australia &New Zealand*, 1987, 3, 5, pp. 515-523.
4. J.R. Bassett & R. Spillane, 'Jet Lag as an Occupational Stressor', *Journal of Occupational Health & Safety – Australia & New Zealand*, 1985, 1, pp. 26-32; J.R. Bassett & R. Spillane, 'Urinary Cortisol Excretion and Mood Ratings in Aircraft Cabin Crew During a Tour of Duty Involving a Disruption in Circadian Rhythm', *Pharmacology, Biochemistry and Behaviour*, 1987, 27, 3, pp. 413-420.
5. M. Wallace (ed.), *Shiftwork in Australia*, Bundoora, La Trobe University: Brain-Behaviour Research Institute, 1985, pp. 10-21.
6. G. Singer, 'Future Options in the Shiftwork Arena', in M. Wallace, ibid., pp. 22-23.

7. M. Wallace (ed.), *Managing Shiftwork*, Bundoora, La Trobe University: Brain-Behaviour Research Institute, 1989, pp. 49-76.

8. J.R. Bassett, P. Marshall & R. Spillane, 'The Physiological Measurement of Acute Stress (Public Speaking) in Bank Employees', *International Journal of Psychophysiology*, 1987, 5, pp. 265-273.

9. J.R. Bassett, B. Hocking & R. Spillane, 'Cortisol Excretion and Illness Reporting: A Psychophysiological Study of Business Executives at Home and at Work', *Journal of Occupational Health & Safety – Australia &New Zealand*, 1998, 14, 2, pp. 135-141.

Chapter 9: Mental Illness as Metaphor

1. F. Marks & B. McLean, *Workers Compensation Law and Practice in New South Wales*, (3rd ed.), North Ryde: CCH Australia, 1992, p. 94.

2. Ibid., p. 190.

3. The story of the medicalising of mental disorders and the battle between the APA and the American Psychological Association is told in S. Kirk & H. Kutchins, *The Selling of DSM: The Rhetoric of Science in Psychiatry*, New York: Aldine De Gruyter, 1992, pp. 111-116.

4. Reark Research, *Community Attitudes to Mental Illness: A Report on Qualitative Research*, Canberra: Department

of Health, Housing, Local Government and Community Services, 1993.

5. R. Spillane, 'Australian Managers' Attitudes to Mental Illness', *Journal of Occupational Health & Safety – Australia & New Zealand*, 1999, 15, 4, pp. 359-364.

6. J. Read, 'Why Promoting Biological Ideology Increases Prejudice against People Labelled "Schizophrenic"', *Australian Psychologist*, 2007, 42, 2, p. 118.

7. F.A. Baughman & C. Hovey, *The ADHD Fraud: How Psychiatry Makes 'Patients' of Normal Children*, Victoria, BC: Trafford Publishing, 2006.

8. For details and reference see, J. Schaler (ed.) *Szasz Under Fire: The Psychiatric Abolitionist Faces His Critics*, Chicago: Open Court, 2004.

Epilogue

1. K.R. Murphy, 'Organisational Psychology's Greatest Hits and Misses: A Personal View', in A.I. Glendon, B.M. Thompson & B. Myors, *Advances in Organisational Psychology*, Bowen Hills, Qld.: Australian Academic Press, 2007, pp. 11-35.

INDEX

Printed in Australia
AUOW01n0001220218
294973AU00004B/4

9 781613 399033